Tom Adams

Exam Practice Workbook

OCR Gateway GCSE Biology B

Contents

1. The table below provides information about blood pressure.

	Systolic (mm Hg)	Diastolic (mm Hg)
Normal blood pressure	Below 120	Below 80
High blood pressure	Above 140	Above 120

Jim is 28. He works in an office and has been promoted to a more responsible job. He works long hours and tends to relax by going to the pub with his mates after work. He had a cold a few months ago but apart from this he is free from infection.

(a) Jim is given a blood pressure meter to monitor his blood pressure on a daily basis. He records his readings as shown.

Day	Monday	Tuesday	Wednesday	Thursday
Blood pressure	142/92	139/89	144/93	142/90

Calculate Jim's average **diastolic** blood pressure. Show your working. [2]

142/91 mm Hg

(b) Jim goes to see the doctor about his blood pressure. Suggest **two** pieces of advice his doctor is likely to give him. [2]

Do more exercise and maintain healthy diet ie less alcohol

(c) Jim decides to get fitter and starts running with his friend Bob. Bob is a regular runner. They fit heart rate monitors to themselves and after exercise Bob finds his heart rate returns to a resting level of 80 bpm within four minutes. Write down how you would expect Jim's monitor information to be different. [2]

Jims heart rate will be higher after exercise and will return back slower & resting heart rate will be higher

(d) Bob says Jim is healthy but not fit. Do you agree with Bob? Explain why. [2]

Yes because health is the absence of disease and fitness is ability to perform exercise he might be absence of disease but no really able to do the fitness components.

2. **(a)** Study the diagram of the artery below. Arteries can become blocked when fatty deposits build up in them. A heart attack results when a component of the blood blocks the vessel at **X.** Name this component. cholesternol [1]

[Total: /9]

Higher Tier

(b) Explain how this leads to a heart attack. In your answer you should include the name of the vessel which becomes blocked and ideas about cardiac muscle and its requirements. [3]

polaiy vien **Vessel blocked** by chloesrnol

Explanation no blood that carries the oxygen can now no longer reach the cardiac muscle in the heart this can lead to a heart attack

3. Carbon monoxide can prevent blood from carrying enough oxygen. Explain how. [2]

the carbon monoxide bines to the haemoglobin better than the oxygen so carbon monoxide gets carried by the blood instead of oxygen.

4. It is important to have a blood pressure as this allows blood to be pumped through the various vessels and reach all tissues of the body. When blood pressure is too high however, this can lead to problems.

(a) Describe **two** problems that can be caused by high blood pressure. [2]

stroke - blood vessels brain burst

kidney failer - blood vessels kidney burst

(b) Describe **one** consequence of having low blood pressure. [1]

fainting

[Total: /8]

1. Karen is determined to improve her lifestyle and make it more healthy. Here is a list of food groups she needs to include for a balanced diet.

carbohydrates **protein** **fats** **vitamins** **minerals**

(a) Ring **two** food groups she should cut down on to reduce her energy intake. [1]

(b) Complete the following sentence. [1]

Vitamin C is important for a healthy diet because

....

(c) A genetic screening shows that Karen might be susceptible to bowel cancer. Write down **one** food group she should **increase** in order to lower her risk. [1]

....

2. The table below provides a guideline for the recommended Body Mass Index.

BMI	What it means
<18.5	Underweight – too light for your height
18.5–25	Ideal – correct weight range for your height
25–30	Overweight – too heavy for your height
30–40	Obese – much too heavy, health risks!

(a) Karen is 1.54 m tall and weighs 66 kg.

The formula for calculating BMI is:

$$\text{BMI} = \frac{\text{mass (kg)}}{\text{height (m)}^2}$$

Use this to calculate Karen's BMI to the nearest whole number. Show your working. [2]

....

(b) Describe what this BMI means for Karen. [1]

....

3. **(a)** Elouise eats 35g of protein per day. She weighs 63kg. Use the equation below to decide whether Elouise is getting enough protein in her diet. [3]

EAR (in g) = 0.6 × body mass (in kg)

....

(b) Elouise is aged 16. Explain why it is especially important for teenagers to have enough protein in their diet. [1]

Because ~~they are~~ growing

[Total: ...... / 10]

Higher Tier

(c) Elouise is a vegetarian. Which phrase describes the type of protein Elouise will eat? Choose from the list.

1st class protein **2nd class protein** **3rd class protein** [1]

2nd class protein

4. The table below shows how obesity in 2–10 year-old children has changed between the years 1995–2003 in the UK.

Year	% of obese children in UK
1995	9.9
1996	10.2
1997	10.8
1998	11.3
1999	11.8
2000	12.3
2001	12.8
2002	13.3
2003	13.7

(a) Predict the percentage obesity for 2004 based on this trend. 14.2% [1]

(b) If the body's daily energy requirements are exceeded, sugar can be converted to storage products, for example fat under the skin. Name **one other** storage product and where it would be found. [2]

carbohydrates ⇒ glucose → glycogen in the liver

[Total: ...... / 4]

1. Draw lines to link the name of the microorganism to the disease or condition it causes. [3]

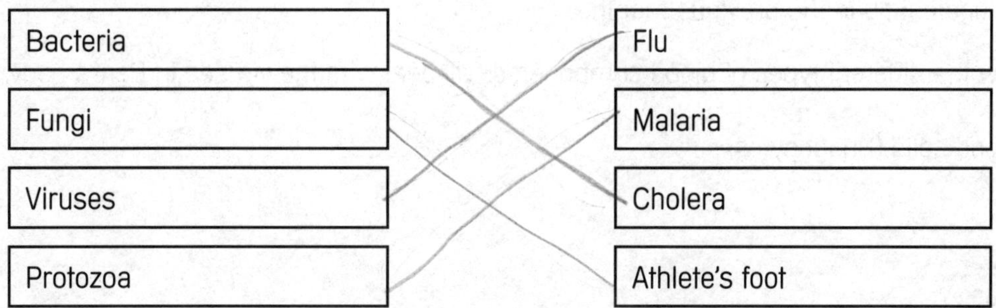

2. Dakoba is a region in Africa where mosquitoes breed rapidly and malaria is very common. Harriet is a British student visiting the region. She notices mosquitoes landing on the skin of babies and sucking their blood. When e-mailing her parents she tells them that parasitic mosquitoes are attacking the babies.

(a) Explain why she is wrong to describe the mosquitoes as parasites. [2]

Because mosquitoes are actually vectors because they carry the parasite and are not effected by it.

(b) Next day, Harriet cuts herself on a dirty stick while making a fire. How will the white blood cells **around the wound** respond? [1]

Make antibodies to fight the invading pathogens

(c) Despite this, some of the bacteria survive and multiply in the wound. Describe how they will harm Harriet's body. [1]

They will release toxic chemicals and harm her cells

3. New drugs have to be carefully tested to check that they are effective and safe. Two methods are animal testing and computer modelling. Give **one advantage** and **one disadvantage** of each type of test. [4]

Drug testing method	Advantage	Disadvantage
Animal testing	It will help us to know if it is harmful before test it on humans	It is considered unethical and cruel.
Computer modelling	No living things are harmed.	we don't know for certain how it will react with live tissue

4. Rani has caught flu and has been confined to bed for several days. Her mother is a health worker and was immunised against flu in the previous month.

(a) Describe how the different types of blood components will deal with the viruses in Rani's body.

(i) White blood cells (Phagocytes) engolts the bacena. [1]

(ii) Antibodies locu onto the antigens on the pathogen and clumps them together [1]

[Total: .... / 13]

Higher Tier

(b) Describe how the cells in Rani's mother's body responded to the vaccination she was given. In your answer state what was in the vaccine and use the words **antigen**, **antibody** and **memory cells**. [4]

antibodies quicky next time

unhalmful flu-pathogen injected into her the white blood cells detect the antigens and make antibodies antibodies locu onto the antigens white blood cell then engulfs them immunity remains in the memory cells which allow white blood cells make

(c) After four days Rani is still unwell and she is taken to the doctor. The doctor advises plenty of rest, regular intake of fluids and painkillers when necessary. Explain why he does not prescribe antibiotics. [2]

Because it antibiotics only work on bacterial infections therefore will not work on virus infections. she would need antiviral

5. What is meant by a **double blind trial**? [2]

when neither the patient nor the doctor know who was the drug and who has the placebo. eliminated biasedness from the doctor

[Total: .... / 8]

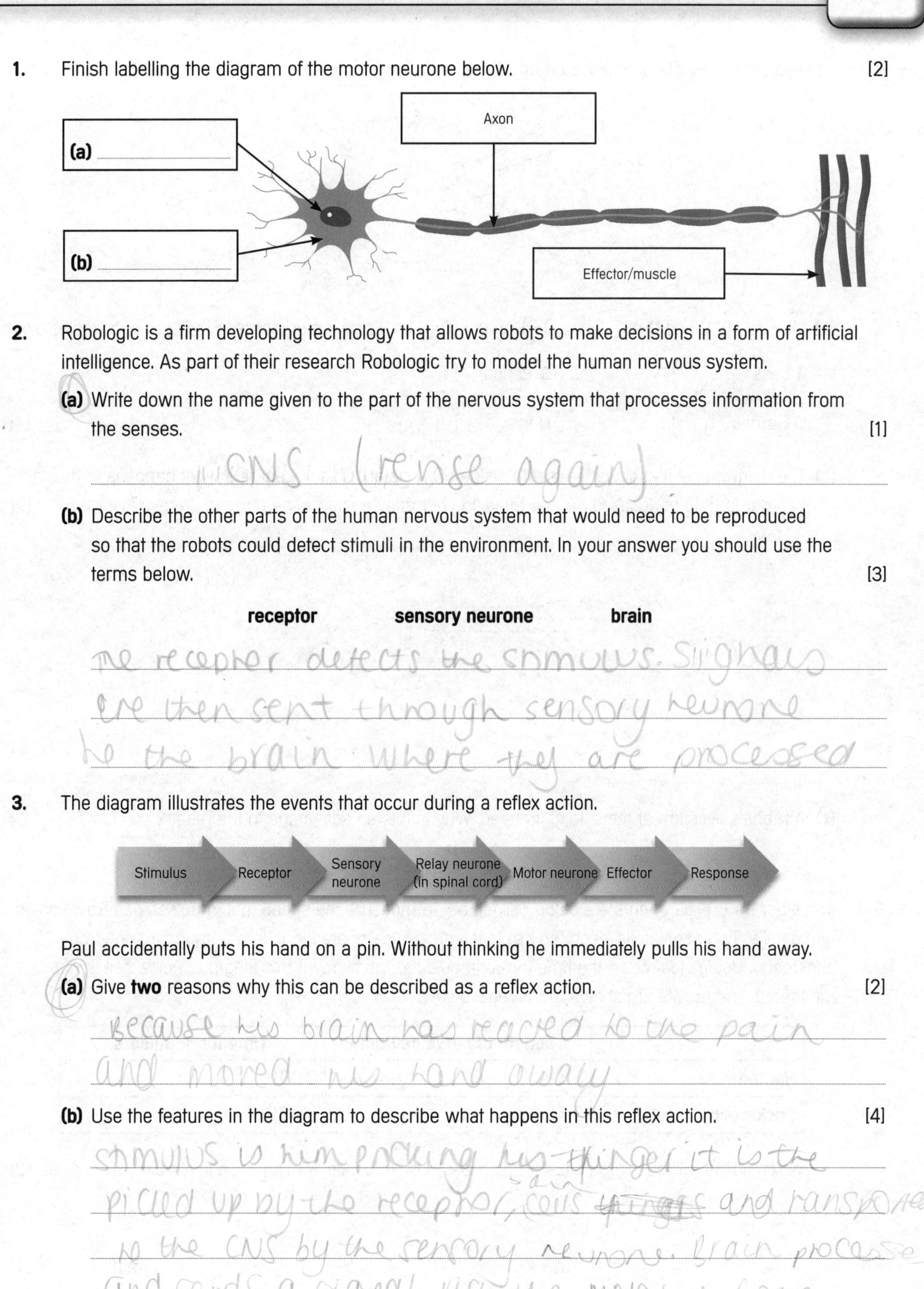

1. Finish labelling the diagram of the motor neurone below. [2]

2. Robologic is a firm developing technology that allows robots to make decisions in a form of artificial intelligence. As part of their research Robologic try to model the human nervous system.

(a) Write down the name given to the part of the nervous system that processes information from the senses. [1]

CNS (sense again)

(b) Describe the other parts of the human nervous system that would need to be reproduced so that the robots could detect stimuli in the environment. In your answer you should use the terms below. [3]

receptor **sensory neurone** **brain**

The receptor detects the stimulus. Signals are then sent through sensory neurone to the brain where they are processed

3. The diagram illustrates the events that occur during a reflex action.

Paul accidentally puts his hand on a pin. Without thinking he immediately pulls his hand away.

(a) Give **two** reasons why this can be described as a reflex action. [2]

Because his brain has reacted to the pain and moved his hand away

(b) Use the features in the diagram to describe what happens in this reflex action. [4]

Stimulus is him pricking his finger it is then picked up by the receptor, cells and transported to the CNS by the sensory neurone. Brain processe and sends a signal via the motor neurone to the effector muscles in him harm response is pulling hand away

4. The eye is an example of a sense organ.

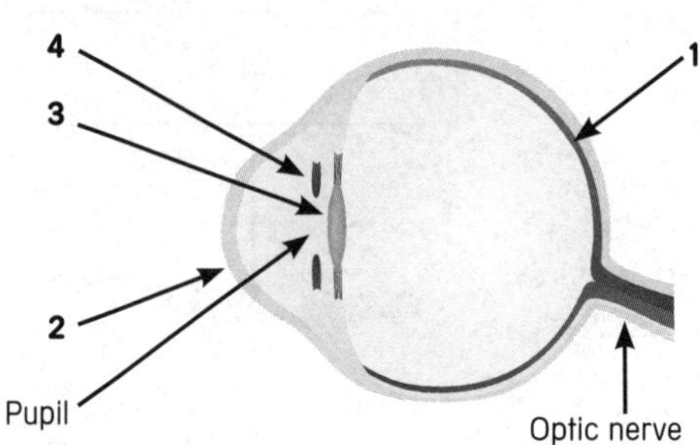

(a) Match **A**, **B**, **C** and **D** with labels **1–4** on the diagram. Enter the numbers in the correct boxes below.

A Lens  3 **B** Retina  1

C Cornea 2 **D** Iris 4  [4]

(b) The diagram below shows the eye focusing on a distant object. Describe what happens to the light in order for it to be focused on the retina. In your answer, name the parts of the eye involved. [2]

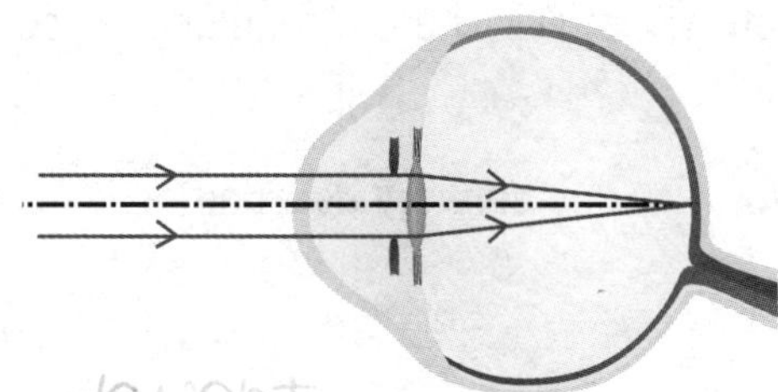

through pupil

cilary muscles taught, suspensory ligaments slack lens goes long and thin light the refracts off the lens onto the retina after refracting off the cornea and going through

(c) A rabbit's eyes are at the side of its head. Why is this an advantage to the rabbit? [1]

wider field of view.

5. In a laboratory, experiments are being carried out to measure the speed that impulses can travel down nerve cells. Two nerve cells, each 3.5 cm in length, are compared, one in a human and one in a cockroach. Using electrodes, the time for an impulse to travel down this length of nerve cell is measured. The results are shown in the table below.

	Length of nerve cell/cm	Time for impulse/s
Human	3.5	0.0015
Cockroach	3.5	0.0019

Which animal do you think has faster responses? Use evidence from the table to explain your answer. [2]

Human because didn't take as long.

[Total: ______ / 21]

Higher Tier

6. The diagram below shows a junction between two nerve cells.

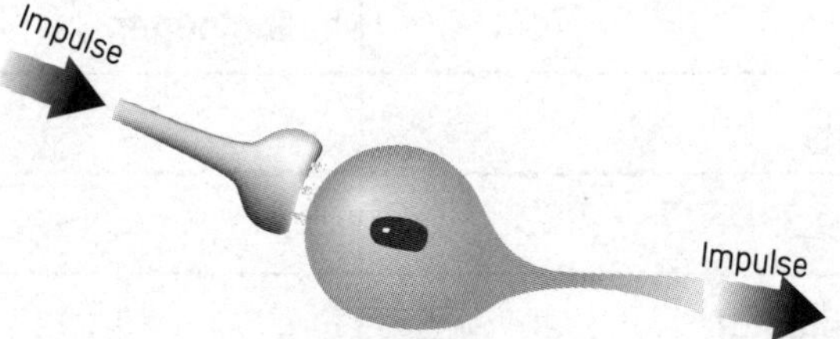

(a) What name is given to this nerve junction? synapse [1]

(b) The nerve cell receiving the impulse is a **motor neurone**. Describe the adaptations of this neurone to the job it does. [3]

Elongated shape to transport impulses quicker

Fatty sheath to insulate pulses stop them crossing over

Branched endings to connect other cells

(c) In order for the impulse to be transmitted from one neurone to the next, a **transmitter substance** needs to be released. Describe the sequence of events involved. [3]

impulse comes to the synapse at
transmitter substance is the release
and carries impulse over the synapse
then binds to the receptors on the
other side and carries along next
neurone

[Total: ...... / 7]

B1 Drugs and You

1. Complete the table below in order to name the group of drugs which each example belongs to. The first one has been done for you. Choose from: [4]

sedative **stimulant** **depressant** **painkiller** **hallucinogen**

LSD	**hallucinogen**
Nicotine	
Alcohol	
Paracetamol	
Tamazepam	

2. **(a)** UK law classifies drugs according to an A, B, C system. Write down **two** ways in which a class A drug would differ from a class C drug. [2]

(b) John has been addicted to heroin for three years now. What does the word **addicted** mean? [1]

(c) As John continues to take heroin, he finds he is becoming more **tolerant** to it. Explain what this means. [2]

(d) Under advice, John is admitted to a rehabilitation centre. While 'coming off' heroin he experiences **withdrawal symptoms**. Name **two** symptoms he might experience. [2]

.... **and** ....

3. The table shows how smoking can affect a person's chances of getting lung cancer.

Number of cigarettes smoked per day	Increased chance of lung cancer compared to non-smokers
5	4 ×
10	8 ×
15	12 ×
20	16 ×

(a) Estimate the increased chance of lung cancer if someone smoked 25 cigarettes per day. [1]

....

(b) Describe and explain how smoking heavily can cause emphysema. [2]

....

....

....

(c) Apart from lung cancer and emphysema, name **one other** disease that can be caused by smoking cigarettes.

.... [1]

[Total: .... / 15]

Higher Tier

4. **Stimulants** and **depressants** both have an effect on nerve junctions. Explain how each behaves. You may use diagrams to help your explanation. [4]

....

....

....

....

....

....

....

....

[Total: .... / 4]

B1 Staying in Balance

1. Rafiq is enjoying a skiing holiday but not the cold! His body works to keep at a constant temperature.

(a) Name the process which governs how conditions are kept constant in the body. [1]

Homostatis

(b) List **two other** conditions which need to be kept constant in the body. [2]

carbon dioxide **and** water

(c) After standing around waiting for a ski lift, Rafiq starts to shiver. Explain how this helps him to conserve heat. [2]

By shivering his muscles are moving so they are respiring generate heat

(d) After skiing cross-country for a while, Rafiq starts to sweat underneath his thermals. Explain how sweating enables him to lose heat. [2]

The sweat cools down the body.

(e) Rafiq's internal body temperature has changed very little during the day. What temperature is this likely to be? Ring the correct answer. [1]

30°C **35°C** **37°C** **40°C** **50°C**

(f) Explain why this temperature needs to be maintained. [1]

Because it is the optamin temp for enzymes

2. Label the gland shown on the diagram and add the name of a hormone it produces. [2]

Gland: pancreas

Hormone: insulin

3. Nanotechnology is a rapidly advancing area of research and makes use of tiny artificial structures down to a molecular level. A new nanotechnology device has been developed for people with diabetes that can detect levels of glucose in the blood and communicate this information to a hormone implant elsewhere in the body. The implant releases a precise quantity of hormone into the bloodstream when required.

(a) Explain how this device could help a person with type 1 diabetes who has just eaten a meal. [2]

....

....

(b) Explain why a person with type 2 diabetes might not have as much use for this technology. [1]

....

4. Study the graph.

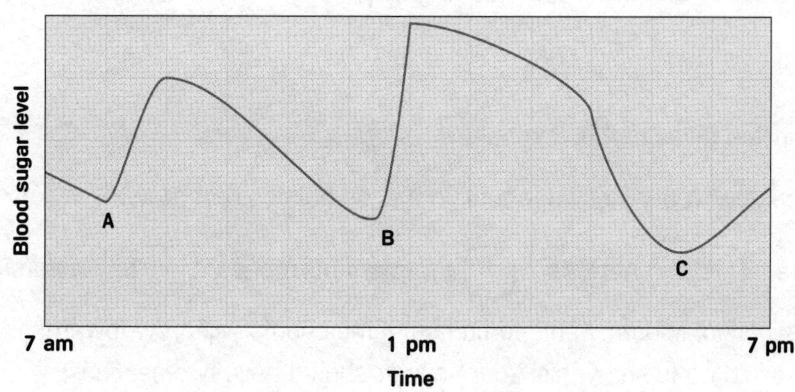

(a) How can we tell from the graph that this person has diabetes? [2]

....

(b) Explain why the person's blood sugar level rises rapidly just after points **A** and **B**. [1]

....

(c) What would have happened after points **A** and **B** if the person did not have diabetes? [1]

....

(d) Why did the person need to eat a chocolate bar at point **C**? [1]

....

[Total: .... / 19]

B1 Controlling Plant Growth

1. This question is about plant growth.

(a) Name **two** factors which plants are sensitive to. [2]

light .... **and** Gravity ....

(b) Miriam is carrying out an investigation into the germination of a broad bean seed. The diagram shows the appearance of a seed she planted after five days. Label the shoot and the root on the diagram. [2]

shoot

root

(c) Describe how the shoot has responded to gravity. [1]

It has moved away ....

(d) What is the name given to this response? Negative geotropic [1]

2. Which substance does rooting powder contain that stimulates root growth? Tick (✓) the correct box.

enzymes ☐ **nitrates** ☐ **plant hormones** ☑ **vitamins** ☐ [1]

3. In another investigation, Miriam wants to find out if the shoots will grow towards the light. Describe an experiment she could do to show this. Your answer should have two sections:

- a method
- the likely results she would get.

✎ *The quality of your written communication will be assessed in this question.* [6]

....

....

....

....

....

....

....

....

....

....

[Total: .... / 13]

1. Draw lines between the boxes to connect each term with the correct definition. [3]

Nucleus	Different forms of the same gene
Chromosomes	Cell structure that contains the chromosomes
Genes	Consist of large numbers of genes
Alleles	Small pieces of DNA that control the development of a characteristic

2. Next to each type of human cell, write down the number of chromosomes it would contain. [3]

Red blood cell .... **Sperm cell** ....

Skin cell .... **Ovum** ....

3. **(a)** George is trying to describe himself. For each feature below, state whether it is caused by **genetics**, the **environment** or a **combination** of both. [4]

(i) 2.01 m tall .... **(ii)** Blue eyes ....

(iii) Blond hair .... **(iv)** Scar on his forehead ....

(v) Speaks German .... **(vi)** 120 kg weight ....

(b) George shares many features with his brother Nathan but he wants to know why he is not identical, even though they have the same parents. Explain to George why this should be so. Use ideas about fertilisation and gametes in your answer. [2]

....

....

....

(c) George has a sister called Olwen. Describe how their sex chromosomes would be different. [1]

....

(d) Olwen was born with a genetic condition called **cystic fibrosis**. George is worried that he might eventually catch this disease. Explain to him why he needn't worry. [2]

....

....

B1 Variation and Inheritance

4. Mary is the owner of two dogs, both of which are about two years old. Both dogs are black in colour and came from the same litter of puppies.

(a) A dog's body cell has 78 chromosomes. How many chromosomes would be in a dog's sperm cells? [1]

39

(b) The dogs' mother had white fur and the father had black fur. Use what you know about genes to explain how these parents could produce puppies with black fur. [2]

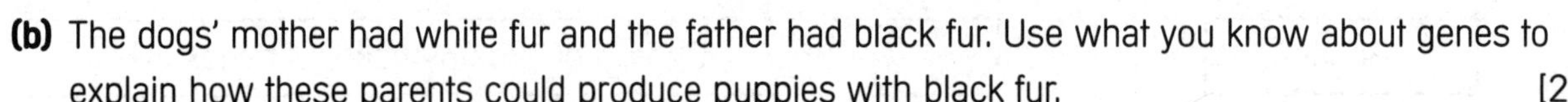

Because the genes would be Bw big be is dominant so they will have black fured babies

white recessive

[Total: .... / 18]

Higher Tier

(c) One year later, one of the black puppies mated with a white-haired dog. She had four puppies. Two had black fur and two had white fur. Draw a fully labelled genetic diagram to explain this. Using the letters **B** and **b** to represent the alleles for fur colour, show which offspring would be black and which would be white. [3]

5. Complete these two different crosses between a brown-eyed parent and a blue-eyed parent. [6]

(a) Brown eyes × Blue eyes

Parents: BB × bb

Gametes

Offspring

(b) Brown eyes × Blue eyes

Parents: Bb × bb

Gametes

Offspring

(c) Explain how parents who both have brown eyes could produce a child who has blue eyes. Use a genetic diagram to help you. [4]

Because they could both carry the recessive blue eyed gene.

6. **(a)** Janine has cystic fibrosis. Her mother and father did not show symptoms of the condition. Using 'c' as the allele for cystic fibrosis, draw a genetic diagram to show how this could occur. [4]

	N	c
N	NN	Nc
c	Nc	cc

(b) What was the probability that Janine's parents would have produced a child with cystic fibrosis? [1]

1/4 25%

(c) Which phrase describes the genotype of Janine's parents? Ring the correct answer.

homozygous dominant **homozygous recessive** **heterozygous** [1]

[Total: / 19]

B2 Classification

1. Which of the following are types of invertebrates? Put a (ring) around the correct answers. [3]

annelids **reptiles** **molluscs** **crustaceans** **fish** **arachnids**

2. The picture shows a 'Liger'. It is the result of interbreeding between a lion and a tiger. The liger is infertile.

(a) Explain why a lion and tiger are classed as separate species. [1]

....

(b) Lions, tigers and leopards are all carnivorous big cats. They all have five toes on their front paws and four toes on their back paws. Their claws can be drawn back to avoid damage. They all roar. Tigers and leopards tend to be solitary animals but lions live in prides of females with one dominant male.

(i) Underline one piece of evidence in the information above that suggests that lions, tigers and leopards are all descended from a common ancestor. [1]

(ii) This table shows the binomial names of four species.

	Genus	Species
Lion	*Panthera*	*leo*
Tiger	*Panthera*	*tigris*
Leopard	*Panthera*	*pardus*
Snow leopard	*Uncia*	*uncia*

Are leopards more closely related to tigers or snow leopards? Explain your answer. [2]

....

....

....

[Total: .... / 7]

Higher Tier

3. Archaeopteryx is an ancient fossilised species of bird. When first discovered, scientists found it hard to classify. Bacteria are organisms which are also hard to classify but for different reasons.

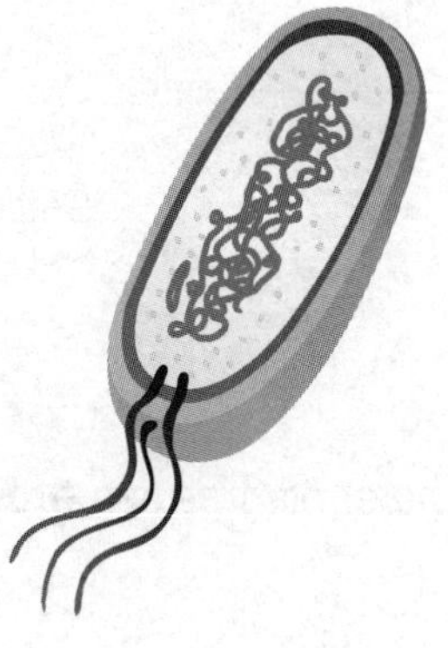

(a) Using features shown in the picture, explain why Archaeopteryx is difficult to classify. [2]

....

....

....

(b) If scientists wanted to determine if one species of bacterium was different from another, what difficulties would they face? [2]

....

....

....

(c) Explain how DNA sequencing might help scientists to classify bacteria. [2]

....

....

....

[Total: .... / 6]

B2 Energy Flow

1. What is represented by the arrow on a food chain? Tick (✓) the correct answer. [1]

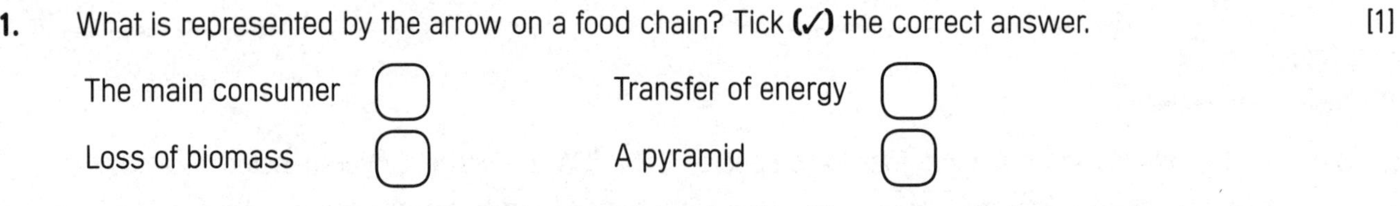

2. Apple trees are grown in orchards in temperate climates. They are part of a wider food web.

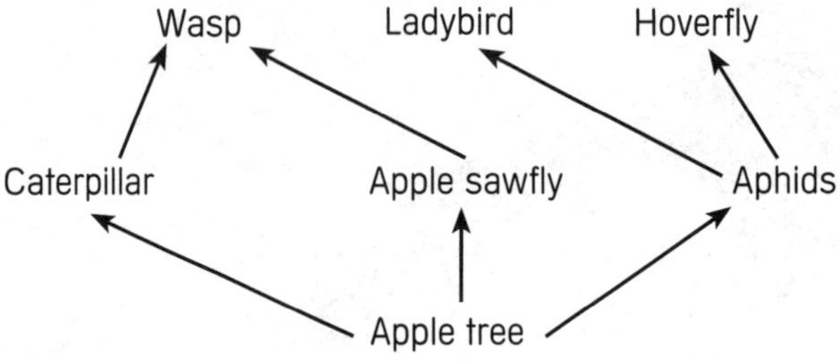

(a) The apple tree is a **producer**. What is meant by this term? [1]

....

(b) What is the source of energy for this food web? .... [1]

(c) Name a secondary consumer in the food web. .... [1]

(d) Below are two pyramids which describe the feeding levels in this food web. Which one accurately shows a **pyramid of biomass**? [1]

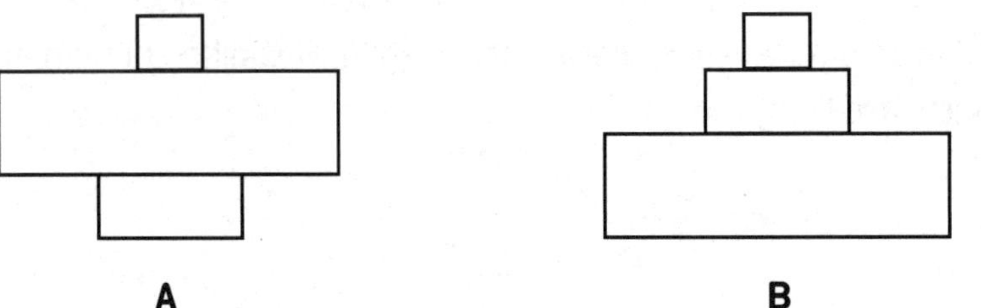

....

(e) Explain how energy can be lost between different feeding levels in the web. [2]

....

....

3. The picture shows the energy intake and use for a cow.

(a) Suggest what form the cow's energy intake is. .... [1]

(b) Suggest the **two** main types of energy that account for the 2000 kJ transferred in the cow. [1]

.... **and** ....

(c) Calculate the energy taken in by the cow which is used for new growth. [1]

....

[Total: .... / 10]

Higher Tier

4. **(a)** Using the formula below, calculate the energy efficiency for the cow. Show your working. [2]

$$\text{energy efficiency} = \frac{\text{energy used usefully for new growth}}{\text{energy taken in}} \times 100\%$$

....

(b) Humans do not need to eat as large a biomass as cows do. Explain why. [2]

....

....

(c) Use the information in answers **(a)** and **(b)** to explain why vegetarianism is more energy efficient than eating meat. In your answer, explain the implications for agricultural land use if significant numbers of a population are vegetarian. [6]

✎ *The quality of your written communication will be assessed in this question.*

....

....

....

....

....

....

....

....

....

....

[Total: .... / 10]

B2 Recycling

1. Carbon is an element found in all living things. It is recycled in the environment in a process called the **carbon cycle**. The main features of this cycle are shown below.

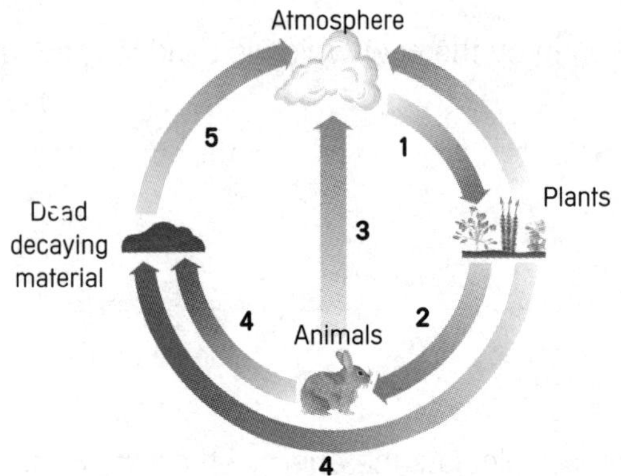

(a) Name the process which occurs at stage **3** in the diagram. .... [1]

(b) The UK government is planning to use fewer fossil-fuel-burning power stations in the future. How might this affect the carbon cycle? Use ideas about **combustion** and **fossil fuel formation** in your answer. [2]

....

....

....

2. Another important process in nature is the **nitrogen cycle.** The diagram below shows the main stages.

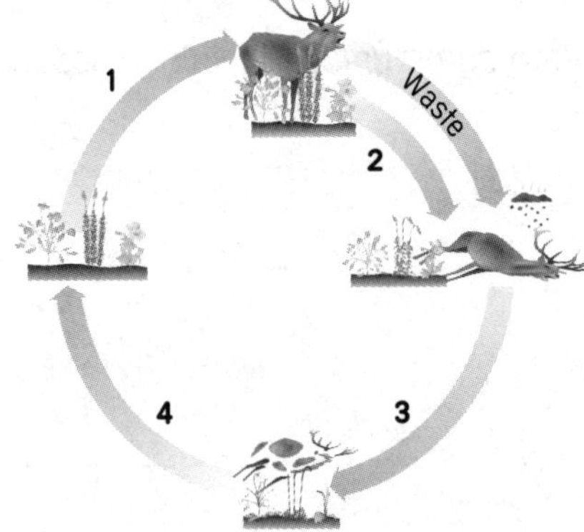

(a) Explain why animals cannot use nitrogen directly from the air. [1]

....

(b) Match processes **A**, **B**, **C** and **D** with the labels **1–4** in the diagram. [2]

A Animals eat plants ☐

B Dead matter is broken down by decomposers ☐

C Plants absorb nitrates from soil ☐

D Death ☐

[Total: .... / 6]

Higher Tier

3. Peat bogs are ancient habitats which can act as **carbon sinks**.

(a) Explain how a peat bog acts in this way. In your answer use ideas about the carbon cycle. [2]

(b) Carbon can also be locked inside limestone. Describe **two** ways in which this carbon can be released once more into the atmosphere. [2]

4. The diagram shows the roots of a pea plant.

(a) Name the type of bacteria that would be found in the root nodules. [1]

(b) Explain why these bacteria are important for the nitrogen cycle. [2]

(c) When animals die and decay, they are acted upon by decomposers. Complete the following equation which describes the decay process.

ammonium compounds $\xrightarrow{\text{nitrifying bacteria}}$ ______________ [1]

(d) Clover is also known to have root nodules. Explain why farmers might want to grow clover every third year in a field which normally contains wheat. [2]

[Total: ______ / 10]

B2 Interdependence

1. The size of a population of swallows found in the South of England was recorded every other summer from 1990.

(a) Draw a graph of the data from the table. [3]

Year	No. of swallows
1990	956
1992	918
1994	876
1996	834
1998	797

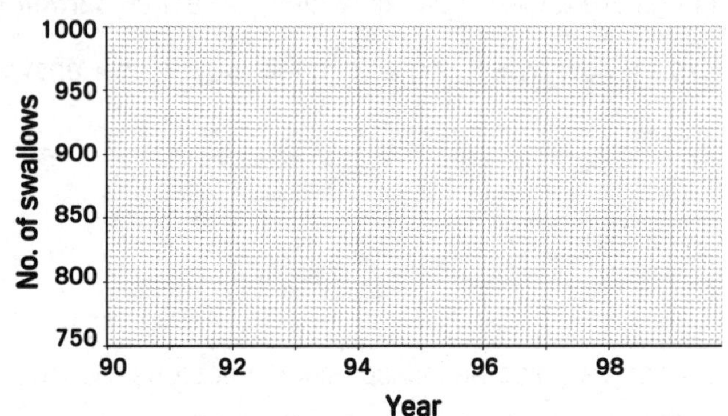

(b) Estimate the size of the swallow population in the summer of 1999. [1]

(c) In 1992, pesticides were introduced in the South of England which reduced the population of flying insects. Suggest how this might be connected with the decline in the number of swallows. [2]

2. The following information on the population of stoats and rabbits in a particular area was obtained over a period of ten years.

Year	1989	1990	1991	1992	1993	1994	1995	1996	1997	1998
No. of stoats	14	8	8	10	12	16	14	6	8	12
No. of rabbits	320	360	450	600	580	410	300	340	450	500

(a) Plot these results onto the graph paper provided. [3]

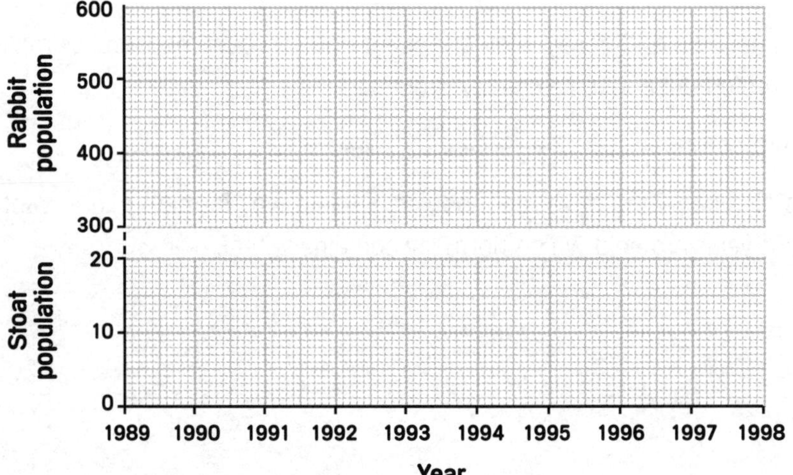

(b) Explain the reason for the variation in the size of the stoat and rabbit populations. [3]

[Total: ____ / 12]

Higher Tier

3. **(a)** Leguminous plants (e.g. peas) have bacteria living in nodules on their roots. How do pea plants benefit from these colonies of nitrogen-fixing bacteria? [2]

(b) What do the bacteria gain from the relationship? [1]

4. Harlequin ladybirds have recently increased in number on the UK's south coast. They occupy the same ecological **niche** as the resident ladybirds.

(a) What is meant by **niche**? [1]

(b) The harlequin ladybird is known to be aggressive. Describe how this is likely to affect the native ladybirds. Use ideas about competition in your answer. [2]

[Total: ____ / 6]

B2 Adaptations

1. This question is about adaptations.

(a) Complete the following passage. Use words from the list. [3]

environment **population** **features** **community** **characteristics**
survival **evolutionary** **predatory** **suited**

Adaptations are special .... or .... which make a living organism particularly well .... to its .... Adaptations are part of an .... process that increases a living organism's chance of ....

(b) Polar bears are found throughout the Arctic. They spend most of their time on ice floes and tend to stay close to the water when on the mainland. Seals form the basis of their diet.

Describe **two** adaptations that help polar bears to survive in the icy wilderness of the Arctic. [2]

....

....

(c) Prey have many adaptations which help them evade predators. The **ibex** (below) is such an animal.

Describe **two** adaptations which would help the ibex evade capture. [2]

....

....

[Total: .... / 7]

Higher Tier

2. A new species of insectivorous mammal has been discovered in Borneo. It was observed in both rainforest undergrowth and more open 'savannah-like' areas. To find out more about it, scientists studied the diet of the creature, which they named a Long-nosed Batink. They obtained this data:

Food	Ants	Termites	Aphids	Beetles	Maggots	Bugs	Grubs
Mass eaten per day/g	275	380	320	75	150	20	110

(a) Plot this data as a bar chart in the grid below. [3]

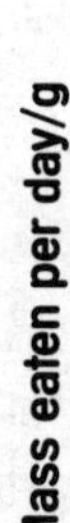

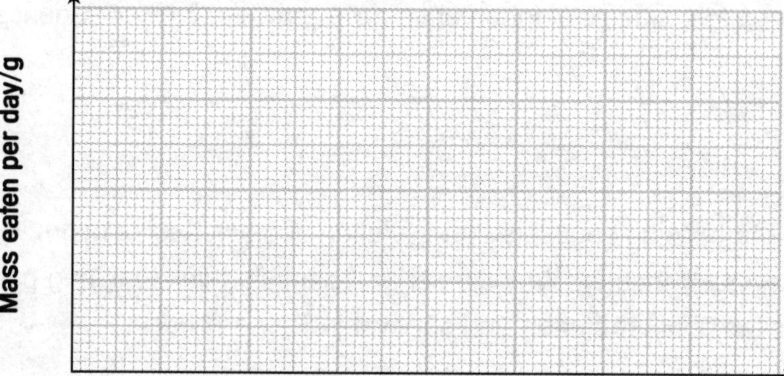

(b) Calculate the **percentage** of the Batink's diet which is made up from **termites.** Show your working. [2]

....

....

(c) The scientists concluded that the Batink had survived many millions of years because of its strategy of being a 'generalist'. Give **two** pieces of evidence from the observations which suggest that the Batink is a generalist. [2]

....

....

[Total: .... / 7]

B2 Natural Selection

1. As the environment changes, species must also change if they are going to survive. Choose the correct words from the options given to complete the following sentences. [2]

selection **adapted** **slow** **genes** **evolved**

Evolution suggests that all living things have .... from simple life forms developed billions of years ago. The process is .... and continual. Evolution enables organisms to become better .... to their environment. Adaptations are controlled by .... and can therefore be passed on to offspring.

2. Neo-Darwinists are scientists who have accepted Darwin's theory of Natural Selection but have built upon it with new ideas. They have developed the theory because of new evidence that has been found.

(a) One of Darwin's main ideas was that successful characteristics can be passed on to the next generation. How might studies of inheritance have provided further evidence for this? [1]

....

....

(b) New evidence and thinking suggests that evolution of new species might happen much more quickly than previously thought. Why did earlier scientists think that long periods of time were needed? Use ideas about **mutation** and **survival** in your answer. [3]

....

....

....

....

(c) Explain how antibiotic-resistant bacteria can arise due to overuse of antibiotics. In your answer use ideas about **variation**, **survival** and **inheritance**. [3]

....

....

....

[Total: .... / 9]

Higher Tier

3. The following data is an estimate of the average number of peppered moths spotted in a survey in the centre of Manchester in the summer months before and after the Industrial Revolution.

	Pre-Industrial Revolution		Post-Industrial Revolution	
Month	**Pale**	**Dark**	**Pale**	**Dark**
June	1261	102	87	1035
July	1247	126	108	1336
August	1272	93	72	1019

(a) Determine the mean number of each colour of moth during the summer and present these figures in the table below. [2]

Pre-Industrial Revolution		Post-Industrial Revolution	
Pale	**Dark**	**Pale**	**Dark**

(b) Draw a bar graph to represent your results. [2]

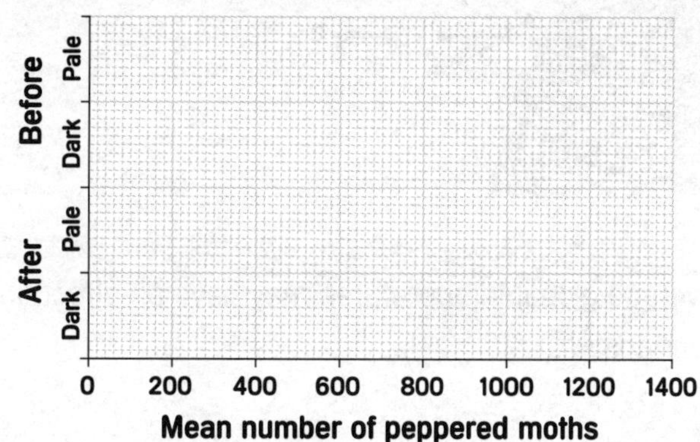

(c) Explain why there were more pale-coloured moths than dark-coloured moths before the Industrial Revolution. [1]

....

(d) Explain why the number of dark-coloured peppered moths increased significantly after the Industrial Revolution. [2]

....

....

....

....

[Total: .... / 7]

B2 Population and Pollution

1. The growing human population is creating three major issues: increased use of finite resources, increased pollution, and increased competition for basic resources. Which of the following are **not** finite resources? Ring all the correct answers that apply. [1]

sea water **wind** **wood** **coal** **minerals** **oil**

2. Images from satellite photography show that there is a hole in the ozone layer.

(a) Name the main gaseous pollutant thought to be responsible for this hole. .... [1]

(b) Explain how a hole in the Earth's ozone layer might lead to increased rates of skin cancer. [2]

....

....

....

3. **(a)** Complete the diagram by labelling the processes involved in the greenhouse effect. [2]

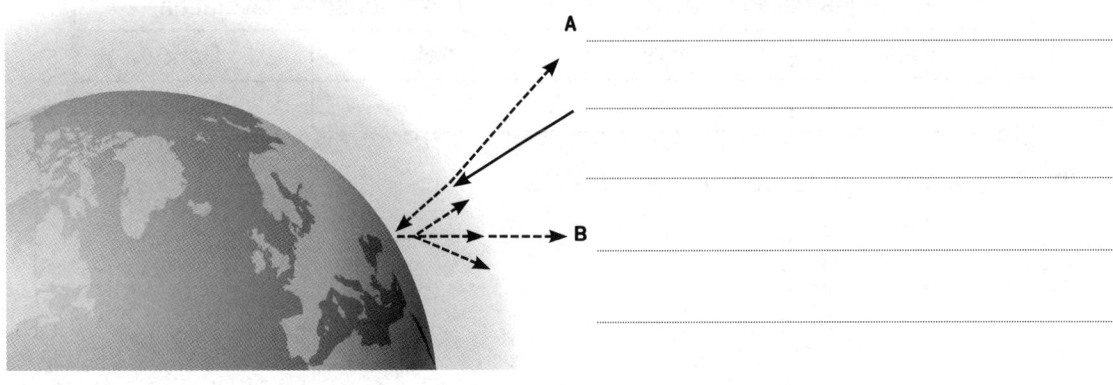

(b) Explain how rising average global temperatures may have an effect on the Earth. Use the headings below to structure your answer. [3]

Climate belts ....

....

Sea levels ....

....

Ice caps and glaciers ....

....

4. A sampling exercise was carried out on a short section of river running by a sewage processing plant. The following results were obtained:

Blood worm	Mayfly nymph	Rat-tailed maggot	Leech	Water louse
4	1	3	2	8

Scientists on the sampling team also measured a pH of 6 in the river water and high nitrate levels.

(a) What is the total population of invertebrates in this sample? .... [1]

(b) What is the total number of species in the sample? .... [1]

(c) The scientists who obtained the sample concluded that the water was slightly polluted. State whether you agree with them or not and give a reason. [2]

Do you agree? **Yes/No** ....

Reason ....

....

(d) What name is given to these invertebrates when used to assess pollution levels? [1]

....

[Total: .... / 14]

Higher Tier

5. At the moment, the human population is increasing exponentially.

(a) Sketch a graph on the axes which shows this increase. [2]

(b) On the *y*-axis, add a suitable unit for the population. [1]

(c) Suggest **two** reasons for this 'population explosion'. [2]

Population/

Time/year

....

....

[Total: .... / 5]

B2 Sustainability

1. The waters around Britain have seen their fish stocks change rapidly since the 1960s. Study the graph below.

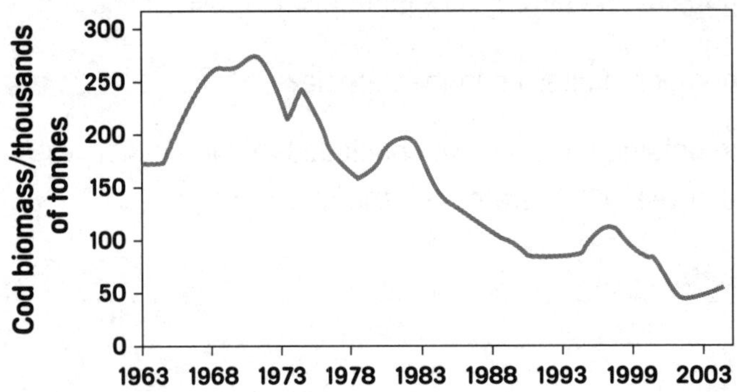

(a) What was the estimated cod biomass in 1978? [1]

.... thousand tonnes

(b) Describe the change in cod numbers between 1978 and 2003. [2]

....

....

(c) International fishing quotas are set in order to manage the numbers of fish in our seas. The table below shows some data about fishing quotas set by an international fishing commission.

Fish species	UK quota 2009/tonnes	UK quota 2010/tonnes
Cod	11,216	13,123
Haddock	27,507	23,381
Whiting	8,426	3,287

(i) By how much did the cod quota change between 2009 and 2010? [1]

.... tonnes

(ii) Suggest possible reasons for the decreased quota for haddock. [2]

....

....

(d) State **one other** measure which fisheries councils can make to prevent over-fishing. [1]

....

2. In Ireland, four species of bumble bee are now designated as endangered. Scientists are worried that numbers may fall so low that they are inadequate to provide pollination to certain plants. State **two** reasons why some organisms become endangered. [2]

....

....

3. People who want to conserve whale species are trying a number of different methods. Describe the **advantages** and **disadvantages** of each method. [6]

Method	Advantages	Disadvantages
Breed whales in captivity in zoos		
Protect natural habitat		
Make whale hunting illegal		

[Total: ...... / 15]

Higher Tier

4. Governments and organisations often have to make balanced decisions about the sustainability of species because the needs of a growing population conflict with this. For each of the following conservation programmes, suggest how human needs might conflict with them.

(a) Placing a ban on hunting rhino in South Africa. [1]

(b) Preventing the burning of moorland heather in Scotland to allow the biodiversity of plants to increase. [1]

(c) Stopping the removal of hedgerows by farmers on agricultural land. [1]

[Total: ...... / 3]

B3 Molecules of Life

1. Muscle cells have many mitochondria.

(a) Explain why there are lots of mitochondria in muscle cells. [2]

(b) There are other structures within cells. Arrange the structures below in order of size, with the largest at the beginning. [1]

gene **nucleus** **cell** **chromosome** **base**

Largest ....

.... Smallest

2.

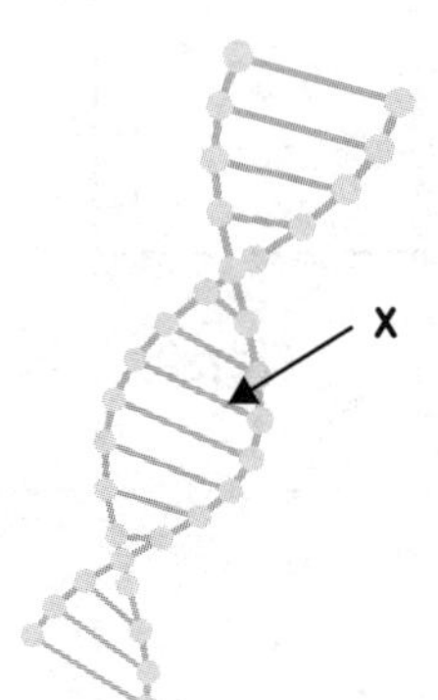

(a) The diagram left shows a molecule of DNA. Name the part labelled **X**. [1]

(b) The 'backbone' of the molecule is arranged in such a way as to make it very stable. Name the term used to describe the shape of DNA.

[1]

[Total: ...... / 5]

Higher Tier

3. **(a)** A team of genetic engineers is analysing DNA fragments. They analyse a section of DNA (right). The compounds which form the rungs of the DNA ladder and code for the structure of protein are arranged in pairs. One strand has been filled in. Write out the matching compounds in the spaces provided. [1]

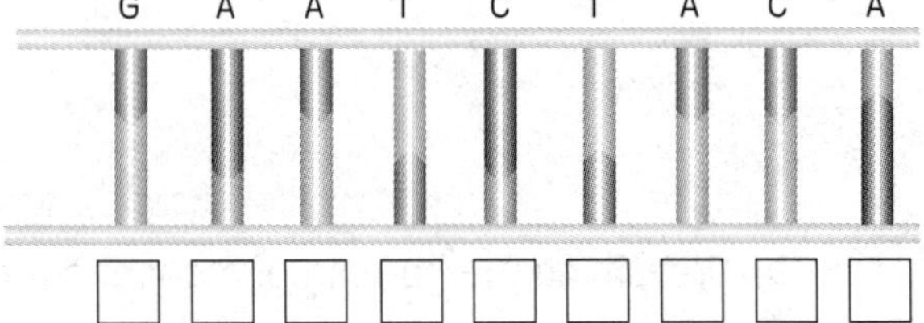

(b) How many of these compounds code for one amino acid? .... [1]

(c) How many amino acids would be coded for by the section of DNA shown? .... [1]

[Total: ...... / 3]

1. In an experiment to investigate the enzyme 'catalase', potato extract was added to a solution of hydrogen peroxide. The catalase in the potato reacted with the hydrogen peroxide and produced oxygen bubbles. The experiment was carried out at different temperatures and the results recorded in the table below.

Temperature/°C	0	10	20	30	40	50	60	70	80
Number of bubbles produced in one minute	0	10	24	40	48	38	8	0	0

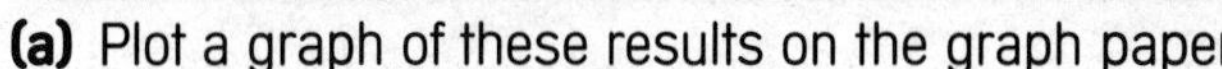

(a) Plot a graph of these results on the graph paper. [3]

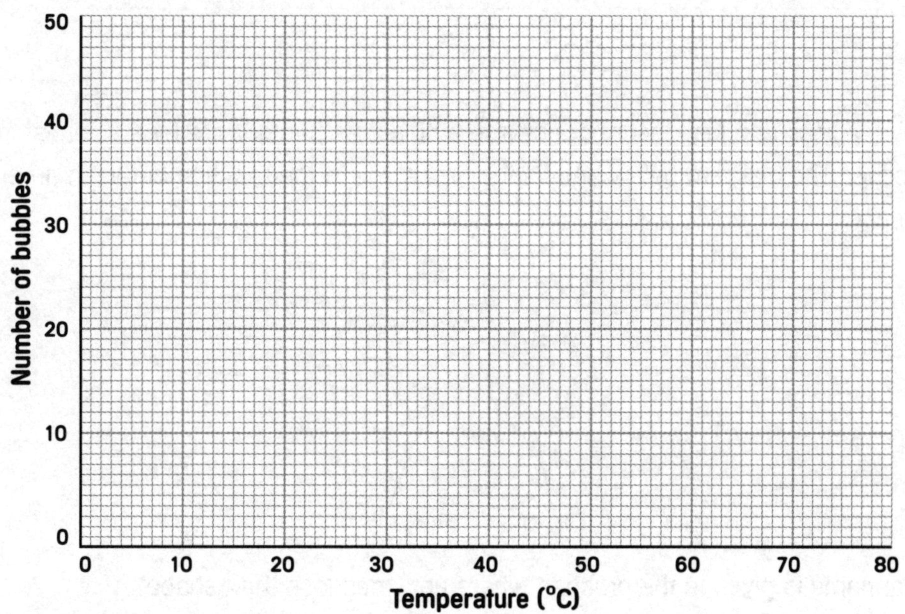

(b) Describe how the number of bubbles produced varies with the temperature of the reacting mixture. [2]

....

....

(c) Using the graph, estimate the **optimum temperature** for catalase to work at. [1]

....

(d) Factors other than temperature affect the activity of enzymes. Explain why the enzyme **amylase,** found in saliva, stops working when it gets to the stomach. [2]

....

....

2. **(a)** Mutations occur when genes on DNA cause them to code for different proteins. State **two** causes of mutation. [2]

.... **and** ....

[Total: .... / 10]

Higher Tier

(b) Explain how a change to a length of DNA might lead to a different protein being formed. You may use a diagram if you wish. [2]

3. In 1894, the 'lock and key' theory of enzyme action was put forward by a scientist called Emil Fischer. The diagram below shows the first stage in the reaction between an enzyme and a reactant.

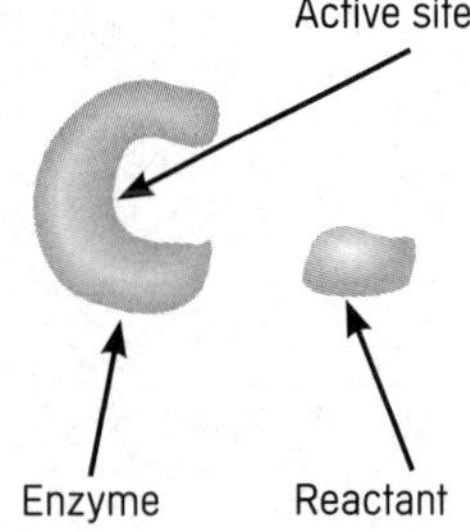

(a) What name is given to the process where enzymes lose their shape? [1]

(b) Use a diagram to explain how the addition of acid will prevent the enzyme from acting properly. [2]

4. At low temperatures, enzymes might not necessarily lose their shape but they still cannot act as quickly. Use the idea of particle theory to explain why. [2]

[Total: ______ / 7]

1. Lisa is playing football. She sprints the length of the field and scores a goal. However, she can barely celebrate because her legs have gone weak and rubbery and she is panting heavily.

(a) Explain why Lisa's legs feel like they do. [2]

(b) Explain why Lisa cannot play the entire game at such a fast pace. [1]

(c) (i) Which type of respiration is more efficient? [1]

(ii) Explain why this type of respiration yields more energy. [1]

2. Larissa is a growing teenager. Her mother notices that her appetite has increased during the last year. She thinks that this is because Larissa needs more energy as she grows.

(a) Describe **two** uses of energy in Larissa's body apart from growth. [2]

and

(b) Describe how Larissa's circulatory system ensures that working cells have enough energy. [2]

3. Isaac is running a marathon. Write a balanced **symbol** equation for the main type of respiration which will be occurring in his muscles. [2]

[Total: / 11]

Higher Tier

4. Isaac's **metabolic rate** is monitored as part of his training schedule. He is rigged up to the metabolic rate meter shown in the diagram over the page. This measures the quantities of gases he breathes in and out. The difference in volume between the inhaled gas and the exhaled gas is proportional to Isaac's oxygen consumption. The microprocessor integrates the signal over the time of the test and multiplies it by a constant to provide a metabolic rate display.

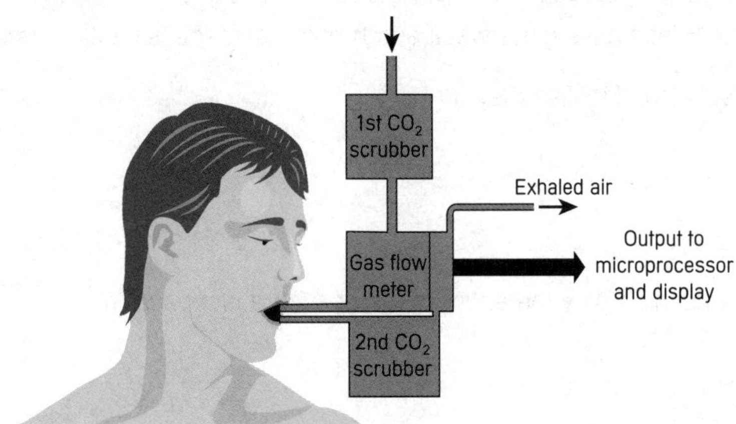

The table below shows some measurements taken from the machine over a period of one hour.

	Five minutes of jogging	Five minutes of rest	Five minutes of sprinting	Five minutes sprinting on an incline
Mean metabolic rate/ml oxygen used per kg/min	35	20	45	60

(a) Explain why a carbon dioxide scrubber is used in the metabolic rate meter. [2]

(b) Why are the figures for metabolic rate adjusted for the body mass of the athlete? [2]

(c) Isaac is quite fit. His friend Boris is not. How might Boris' readings compare with Isaac's? Give a reason for your answer. [2]

(d) Explain the difference in readings for jogging and sprinting. [2]

(e) Isaac was rigged up to the machine again. This time the temperature of the room was raised by 5°C. Describe and explain how Isaac's oxygen consumption rate might change if he was asked to jog again for five minutes. [2]

[Total: .... / 10]

1. The illustrations show a single-celled organism, called an amoeba, and a multi-cellular organism (a horse). Explain why the horse has specialised organs in its breathing and digestive system whereas the amoeba has none. [2]

....

....

....

....

2. Complete the following table which compares the processes of **mitosis** and **meiosis.** [3]

Mitosis	**Meiosis**
Involved in asexual reproduction	
	Produces variation
Produces cells with 46 chromosomes	

3. Insert words in the gaps to complete the following sentences. Choose from the list below. [3]

zygotes **gametes** **diploid** **haploid** **mitosis** **meiosis**

Eggs and sperm are .... They are .... because they contain only one set of chromosomes. Eggs and sperm are produced in the ovaries and testes by ....

4. This question is about causes of variation. Put a tick (✓) next to the **two** statements which are true. [1]

Meiosis shuffles genes which make each gamete unique. ☐

Gametes fuse randomly. ☐

Sperm exchange genes between each other. ☐

The zygote has some bases removed when it enters the uterus. ☐

The DNA molecule mutates regularly in the growing embryo. ☐

[Total: .... / 9]

Higher Tier

5. John is studying chicken cells and is looking at some examples down the microscope. He draws these cells (right).

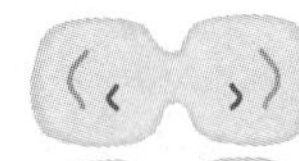

(a) Which type of cell division is shown here? [1]

(b) Give a reason for your answer to **(a)**. [1]

6. John wants to find out what happens to DNA molecules during cell division. Complete the flow diagram below to complete the sequence which DNA molecules go through when they replicate. [2]

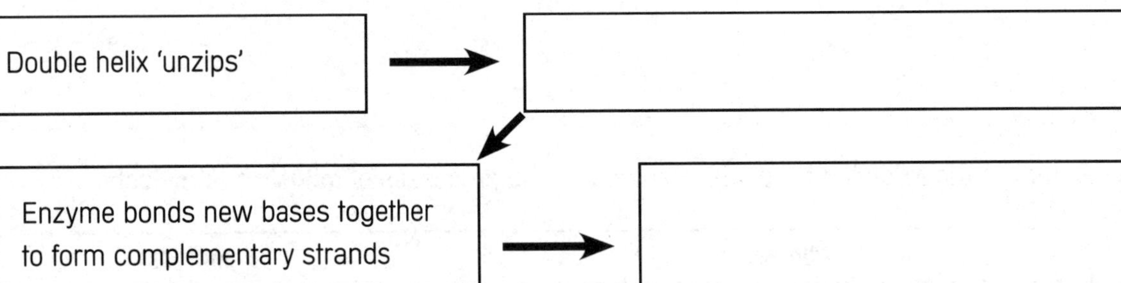

7. The diagrams show a neurone (left) and a collection of red blood cells (right). There are many other different types of cells found in humans which all arose from the same basic type in the early embryo.

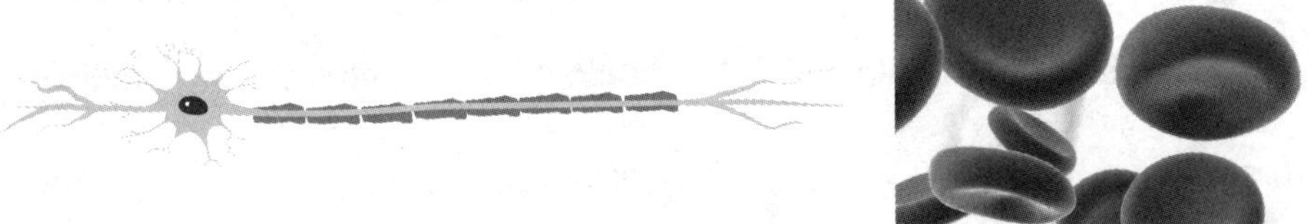

(a) Name the process by which these cells became specialised. [1]

(b) The red blood cells form one tissue in the circulatory system, which is used for transport. Explain why a human has these specialised cells but a paramecium (single-celled organism) does not. [2]

[Total: ____ /7]

1. A software designer has been given the brief as part of a team to produce a computer program that mimics the behaviour of the human circulatory system. The program will contain animations and questions for students to answer.

(a) The designer has set the following introductory question about the components of blood.

The blood is a liquid tissue, which has a variety of jobs to do. Four components of blood are shown in the table. Complete the table by entering the function of each component. [3]

Component	Function
Plasma	
White blood cell	
Red blood cell	
Platelet	

(b) The next part of the program produces an animation of the heart and major blood vessels. One animator uses the diagram below to base the animation on.

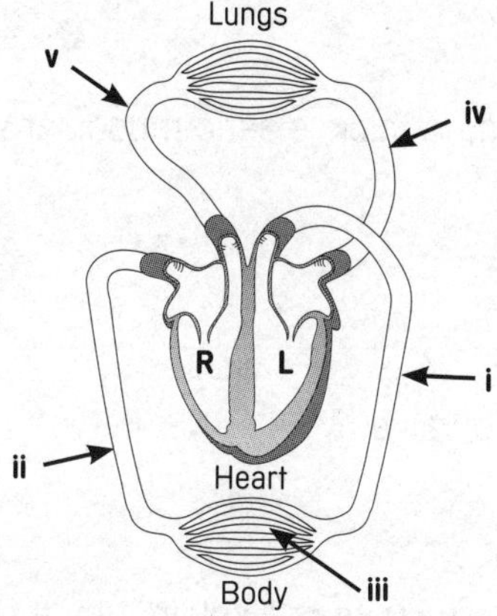

In order to show the blood flow correctly he adds some labels to the diagram. Add an arrow above **R** and one above **L** to show the animator which direction the blood flows in. [2]

(c) The content author needs to indicate which vessels carry oxygenated blood. Ring the correct vessels shown below. [1]

i **ii** **iii** **iv** **v**

(d) Give a biological reason why the animator has to show the left side of the heart as more muscular than the right. [1]

B3 The Circulatory System

2. A student draws a blood vessel. Its diameter is 5 cm. He is viewing the vessel under a microscope at x 40 magnification. Calculate the actual diameter of the blood vessel. Show your working. [2]

....

....

[Total: .... / 9]

Higher Tier

3. The diagrams show two types of blood vessel.

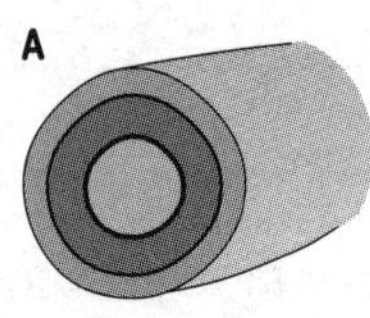

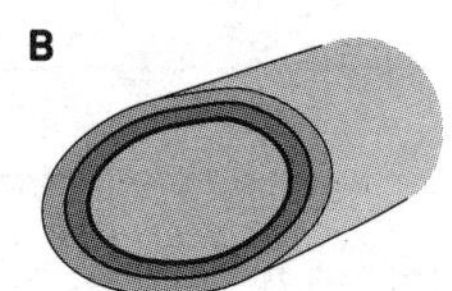

(a) Name each type of blood vessel. [2]

A .... **B** ....

(b) Explain why blood vessel **A** has a thick, elastic muscular wall. [1]

....

....

(c) Why does blood vessel **B** have valves? [1]

....

4. Mammals have a **double circulatory system.** Explain why this is an **advantage** over a single circulatory system. [1]

....

5. Red blood cells contain haemoglobin which absorb oxygen. Complete the word equation below to show what happens in this process. [2]

.... + oxygen $\rightleftharpoons$ ....

[Total: .... / 7]

1. This diagram is of a typical plant cell. Match terms **A, B** and **C** with the labels **1–3** on the diagram. Enter the numbers in the boxes provided. [3]

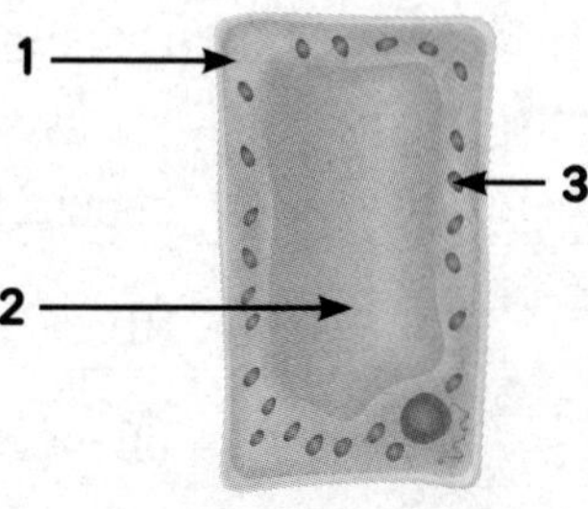

A Chloroplast ☐ **B** Vacuole ☐ **C** Cell wall ☐

2. **(a)** Describe what a stem cell is. [2]

....

....

(b) State **two** uses of stem cells. [2]

.... **and** ....

3. This graph shows the general growth pattern for an organism.

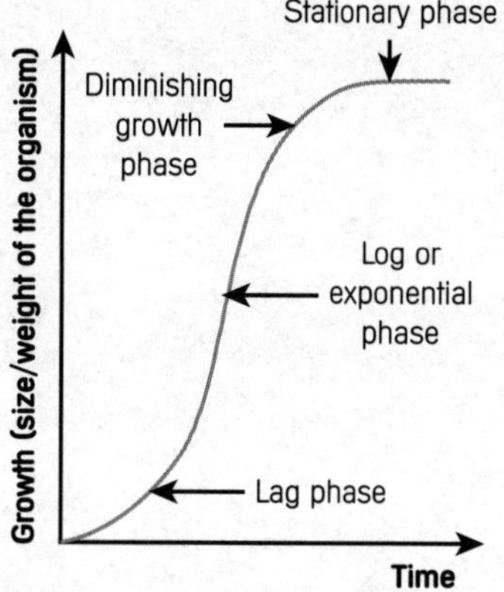

(a) In which phase shown on the graph does most rapid growth occur? .... [1]

(b) What is happening to growth during the **stationary** phase? [1]

....

(c) What name is given to this type of graph? .... [1]

4. Young children grow very quickly up to the age of two years and then their rate of growth slows down. They have another growth spurt during adolescence.

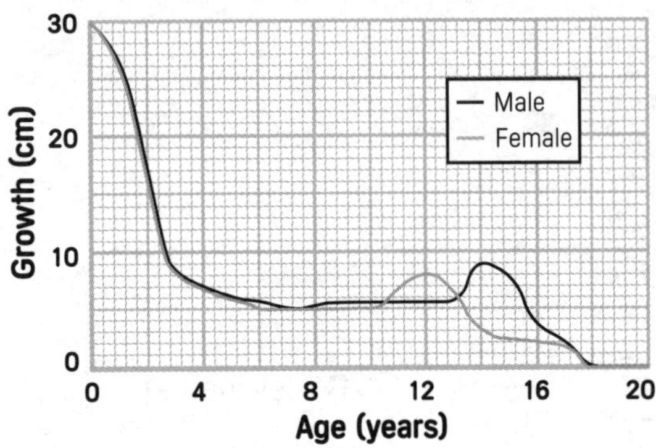

(a) Use the graph to find the age at which the average adolescent growth spurt occurs for . . . [2]

(i) girls ....

(ii) boys ....

(b) Why is there a difference between girls and boys? [1]

....

5. Large numbers of embryos are grown by scientists to obtain stem cells for research. The technique is called ***in vitro* fertilisation.** Only some of these embryos are used for infertile couples. The rest are used for research. Discuss the **advantages** and **disadvantages** of using stem cells for research.

✏ *The quality of your written communication will be assessed in this question.* [6]

....

....

....

....

....

....

....

....

....

....

[Total: .... / 19]

Higher Tier

6. Describe how the DNA in a bacterial cell is different from that in a plant cell. [2]

....

[Total: .... / 2]

1. The appearance of wheat plants has changed significantly in the last few hundred years.

(a) Look at the diagrams. State **two advantages** of a modern-day wheat plant over its ancestor. [2]

(b) Describe **one** additional characteristic that would be useful for modern-day wheat plants to possess. [1]

2. (a) A farmer wants to modify his milk yield to get high volumes of creamy milk that he can sell to ice cream makers. At the moment, he keeps two different breeds of cow: one produces a lot of low-cream milk, the other breed produces small amounts of high-cream milk. Describe the selective breeding process the farmer should go through to get cows which produce large volumes of creamy milk. [3]

(b) Apart from dairy production, state **one other** characteristic which farmers might want to select in cattle. [1]

3. Genetic engineering is another method by which man can obtain genetically different organisms. Describe how genetic engineering is different from selective breeding. [2]

4. Below are two examples of genetic engineering. For each, explain the **advantage** such modification brings.

(a) Resistance to herbicide in soya plants. [1]

....

....

(b) Inserting beta-carotene genes into rice plants. [1]

....

....

5. Genetic engineering opens up a number of possibilities for the human race, as well as many possible dangers. Discuss whether scientists should continue their research. Include at least **three disadvantages** or **three advantages**. [3]

....

....

....

[Total: .... / 14]

Higher Tier

6. The schematic below shows how insulin can be genetically engineered.

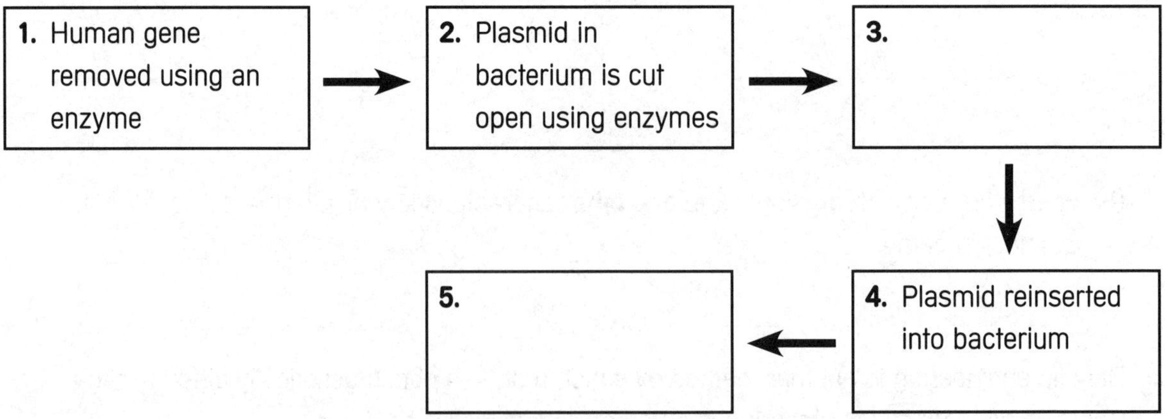

1. Human gene removed using an enzyme →	**2.** Plasmid in bacterium is cut open using enzymes →	**3.**
	5. ←	**4.** Plasmid reinserted into bacterium

(a) Write in the missing steps **3** and **5**. [2]

(b) Name the type of enzyme used in steps **1** and **2**. .... [1]

[Total: .... / 3]

1. **(a)** Cloning can occur naturally when organisms reproduce asexually. Which type of cell division is involved in natural cloning? [1]

....

(b) Suggest why this type of reproduction could be useful to commercial plant growers. [1]

....

(c) Describe **two disadvantages** of commercial cloning. [2]

....

....

....

....

2. One reason for cloning animals would be to supply organs for transplants in humans. The animals would have to be genetically modified first.

(a) Explain why you cannot transplant a normal pig's kidney into a human patient. [1]

....

(b) It is technically possible, although illegal, to clone human embryos beyond 14 days old.

(i) Give **one** reason why this might be **desirable**. [1]

....

....

(ii) Give **one** reason why this might be **undesirable**. [1]

....

....

[Total: .... / 7]

Higher Tier

3. The diagram below shows the three stages involved in tissue culturing.

1 

2  

3   

Describe the procedures involved in stages **1–3**. [3]

Stage 1 ....

Stage 2 ....

Stage 3 ....

4. Dolly the sheep was cloned as an adult. Farmers could gain much from this type of cloning. Describe **two benefits** and **two risks** of adult cloning. [4]

Benefits ....

....

Risks ....

....

[Total: .... / 7]

OCR Gateway GCSE Biology B Workbook Answers

Answering Quality of Written Communication Questions

A number of the questions in your examinations will include an assessment of the quality of your written communication (QWC). These questions are worth a maximum of 6 marks and are indicated by a pencil icon (✐).

Your answers to these questions will be marked according to...
- the level of your understanding of the relevant science
- how well you structure your answer
- the style of your writing, including the quality of your punctuation, grammar and spelling.

QWC questions will be marked using a 'Levels of Response' mark scheme. The examiner will decide whether your answer is in the top level, middle level or bottom level. The expected quality of written communication is different in the three levels and it will always be considered at the same time as looking at the scientific information in your answer:
- To achieve Level 3 (which is the top level and is worth 5–6 marks), your answer should contain relevant science, and be organised and presented in a structured and coherent manner. You should use scientific terms appropriately and your spelling, punctuation and grammar should have very few errors.
- For Level 2 (worth 3–4 marks), there may be more errors in your spelling, punctuation and grammar, and your answer will miss some of the things expected at Level 3.
- For Level 1 (worth 1–2 marks), your answer may be written using simplistic language. You will have included some relevant science, but the quality of your written communication may have limited how well the examiner can understand your answer. This could be due to lots of errors in spelling, punctuation and grammar, misuse of scientific terms or a poor structure.
- An answer given Level 0 may contain insufficient or irrelevant science, and will not be given any marks.

You will be awarded the higher or lower mark within a particular level depending on the quality of the science and the quality of the written communication in your answer.

Even if the quality of your written communication is perfect, the level you are awarded will be limited if you show little understanding of the relevant science, and you will be given Level 0 if you show no relevant scientific understanding at all.

To help you understand the criteria above, three specimen answers are provided to the first QWC question in this workbook. The first is a model answer worth 6 marks, the second answer would be worth 4 marks and the third answer worth 2 marks. The three exemplar answers are differentiated by their scientific content and use of scientific terminology. Model answers worth 6 marks are provided to all other QWC questions to help you aspire to the best possible marks.

B1: Understanding Organisms

Pages 3–4

1. **(a)** $\frac{364}{4} = 91$
   (1 mark for correct answer, 1 mark for showing working.)
   (b) **Any two from**: Decrease alcohol intake; Reduce stress; Work fewer hours; Reduce salt intake; Reduce fat intake in diet.
   (c) Resting rate higher; Time for pulse to return to resting rate is longer.
   (d) YES – Jim is free from infection, but his heart monitor information shows that he is not as capable of carrying out physical exercise as Bob.
   Or NO – Jim is neither fit nor healthy as his physical well-being is limited by high blood pressure/prone to heart disease.
2. **(a)** Thrombus **or** thrombosis
   (b) **Vessel blocked**: Coronary artery **(1 mark)**
   Explanation: Oxygen/glucose is prevented from reaching the heart muscle; So the heart muscle dies/becomes scarred/can no longer respire.
3. Carbon monoxide combines irreversibly with haemoglobin, in red blood cells/carbon monoxide has a higher affinity for oxygen; Oxygen can no longer bind with haemoglobin/enter red blood cell.
4. **(a)** **Any two from**: Burst blood vessels; Damage to brain; Stroke; Kidney damage; Heart attack.
   (b) **Any one of**: Dizziness; Fainting; Poor circulation.

Pages 5–6

1. **(a)** Carbohydrates **and** fats **should be ringed. (Both required for 1 mark.)**
   (b) Vitamin C is important for a healthy diet because it prevents scurvy and is essential for healthy skin and gums.
   (c) Fibre
2. **(a)** $\frac{66}{1.54^2} = 28$ (to nearest whole number). **(1 mark for correct answer, 1 mark for showing working.)**
   (b) Karen is slightly overweight so she needs to lose some weight.
3. **(a)** $0.6 \times 63 = 37.8$ g **(1 mark for correct answer, 1 mark for showing working.)** Elouise should eat at least 2.8 g more **(1 mark)**.
   (b) Protein is needed for growth and teenagers grow rapidly.
   (c) 2nd class protein
4. **(a)** Value estimated between 14.0% and 14.3%.
   (b) Storage product is glycogen; Found in liver/muscles.

Pages 7–8

1. Bacteria – Cholera; Fungi – Athlete's foot; Viruses – Flu; Protozoa – malaria. **(Four correct = 3 marks, subtract 1 mark for every incorrect link, subtract 1 mark for multiple lines.)**
2. **(a)** Mosquitoes are vectors; Which transfer the malaria/parasite (a protozoan).
   (b) Engulf/digest bacteria.
   (c) Damage Harriet's cells/produce toxins.
3. **Animal testing**
   Advantage: Any one of: Chosen animals, e.g. mice, have similar organs and systems to humans so make good models; Can screen potential problems with side effects.
   Disadvantage: Any one of: Many people think this is cruel and does not respect animal life; Animal systems may respond differently to human systems.
   Computer modelling
   Advantage: Any one of: Does not involve a living organism; Low cost – animals not involved.
   Disadvantage: Can only predict effect of new drugs based on knowledge of old ones.
4. **(a)** **(i)** Phagocytes engulf pathogen, then digest it **(1 mark)**.
   (ii) Antibodies lock on to antigen/pathogen/Clump pathogens together **(1 mark)**.

(b) The vaccine contains dead/heat-treated pathogen/microbe. **(1 mark)**
Any three from: Antigen recognised as foreign/non-self; Lymphocytes produce antibodies against it; Memory cells (specialised white blood cells) remain in system; Ready to produce antibodies if re-infection occurs.
(c) Antibiotics do not work against viruses; Over-prescription may lead to resistant bacteria.

5. Subjects of experiment do not know whether they are receiving the active ingredient or the placebo; Scientists, e.g. doctors, do not know who they are administering the active ingredient and the placebo to.

Pages 9–11

1. (a) Nucleus
(b) Cell body **or** cytoplasm.
2. (a) Central nervous system
(b) Receptors sense/detect stimuli; And transfer nervous information/impulses through sensory neurones; To the brain.
3. (a) The response is automatic/unconscious; Response is rapid.
(b) **Any four from**: Sensor/(pain) receptor detects stimulus/pin; Sensory neurone transmits impulse to CNS/spine; Relay neurone passes impulse on; Impulse sent down motor neurone; To effector/arm muscle.
4. (a) **A**–3; **B**–1; **C**–2; **D**–4
(b) Light rays fall on the cornea where they are refracted/bent; The lens then refracts/bends light further.
(c) Enables rabbits to have an almost 360° view to detect approaching predators.
5. Human **(no marks)**; Time for impulse to travel in human is quicker/lower; By 0.00014 s/Compare 0.0015 s in human with 0.0019 s in cockroach.
6. (a) Synapse
(b) **Elongated shape** to carry impulses over long distances; **Fatty sheath** to speed up nervous transmission; **Branched endings** to make connections with many other nerve cells.
(c) **Any three from**: Transmitter substance released at end of 1st neurone in response to impulse; Travels across synaptic cleft by diffusion; Transmitter binds with receptor molecules on next neurone; Impulse released in 2nd neurone.

Pages 12–13

1. Nicotine – stimulant; Alcohol – depressant; Paracetamol – painkiller; Tamazepan – sedative.
2. (a) A class A drug carries higher penalties; Class A drugs are deemed to be more harmful.
(b) A psychological or physical need for something which makes you want more of it (a craving).
(c) He has to use larger amounts; To get the same effects.
(d) **Any two from**: Psychological problems; Sweating; Stomach cramps; Shaking; Nausea; Cravings.
3. (a) 20 x
(b) **Any two from**: Cigarette smoke causes alveoli/air sac walls to collapse; Lower surface area slows down diffusion rate for gases; Gaseous exchange less efficient; Therefore person becomes breathless.
(c) **Any one of**: Bronchitis; Heart disease; Stroke.
4. **Stimulants**: **A description or diagram to show**: Stimulant increasing production of transmitter substance; Increasing level of activity in nervous system.
Depressants: **A description or diagram to show any two from**: Depressant binding with receptor molecule in synapse; Blocking transmission of impulse; Leads to lower nervous system activity.

Pages 14–15

1. (a) Homeostasis
(b) Blood sugar; Water
(c) **Any two from**: Muscle contraction; Generates heat; Through respiration.
(d) **Any two from**: Evaporation of water from skin; Takes in heat from skin; Radiation; Endothermic change.
(e) 37°C
(f) To enable enzymes to work at their optimum temperature.
2. **Gland**: pancreas, **Hormones**: insulin
3. (a) Hormone controls insulin; Which can control blood sugar level.
(b) People with type 2 diabetes can often control their sugar levels by adjusting their diet.
4. (a) The person's blood sugar level **(1 mark)** fluctuates dramatically **(1 mark)**.
(b) The person will have eaten their breakfast and dinner at points **A** and **B** respectively.
(c) There would have been a slight rise, followed by a swift drop back to the normal level.
(d) Because their blood sugar level dropped.

Page 16

1. (a) Light; Gravity
(b) The upper extension is the shoot **(1 mark)** and lower extension is the root **(1 mark)**.
(c) It is growing against the force of gravity.
(d) Negative geotropism **or** negative gravitropism.
2. Plant hormones **should be ticked**.
3. **This is a model answer which would score the full 6 marks:**
Miriam would take 100 seeds of the same mass and grow them in two trays of the same compost with an equal spacing between them. One tray would be put in a dark place with a single light source (e.g. lamp) shining from one direction. The other tray (the control) would be put in a place with plenty of light. Over five days she would give both trays of shoots equal measures of water. After five days the seeds with shoots are removed. Miriam would find that most, if not all, the shoots in the first tray had grown towards the lamp (light source) and the shoots in the second tray would have grown vertically. The experiment could be repeated to increase the reliability of the observations.
This answer would score 4 marks: Miriam would take 100 seeds and plant them in two trays. One tray would be in a dark place and have a lamp shining on it and the other would be in lots of light. She would water both trays. After five days she would find that the shoots in the first tray grow towards the light source and the shoots in the second tray grow straight up.
This answer would score 2 marks: Miriam would plant 100 seeds in trays. One tray would have a lamp shining on it and the other would be in lots of light. After a few days the plants in the first tray will have grown towards the lamp.

Pages 17–19

1. Nucleus – Cell structure that contains the chromosomes
Chromosomes – Consist of large numbers of genes
Genes – Small pieces of DNA that control the development of a characteristic
Alleles – Different forms of the same gene
(3 marks for four correct answers, subtract 1 mark for every incorrect link, subtract 1 mark for multiple lines.)
2. Red blood cell – 0; Sperm cell – 23; Skin cell – 46; Ovum – 23
(All correct = 3, subtract 1 for every incorrect response.)
3. (a) **(i)** Combination; **(ii)** Genetics; **(iii)** Combination; **(iv)** Environment; **(v)** Environment; **(vi)** Combination **(4 marks for all correct, subtract 1 mark for every incorrect response.)**
(b) George and Nathan's parents produced many unique/genetically different gametes; These gametes randomly fused/joined during fertilisation.
(c) Olwen has XX, George has XY.
(d) Cystic fibrosis is inherited, not infectious; Can only be transferred from parents.
4. (a) 39
(b) Black is the dominant gene/allele/White is recessive **(1 mark, note: not given for references to 'black chromosome' or 'white chromosome')**; The gene for black fur is passed on/inherited **from the father (1 mark)**.

(c) **1st mark for**: correct genotype for both parents Bb and bb or correct gametes Bb and bb; **2nd mark for**: genotype of offspring correct Bb and bb; **3rd mark for**: showing correct phenotype of offspring **(see below in terms of diagrams)**.

	b	**b**
B	Bb Black	Bb Black
b	bb White	bb White

Or

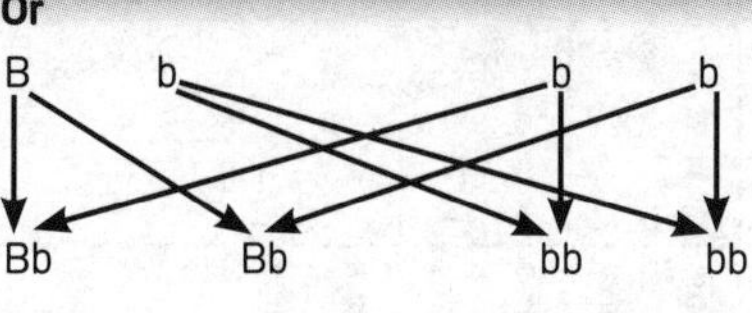

Black Black white white

5. **(a)** Brown eyes × Blue eyes

Parents BB bb

Gametes B B b b

Offspring Bb Bb Bb Bb

Brown	Brown	Brown	Brown

(1 mark will be awarded for each correct row.)

(b)

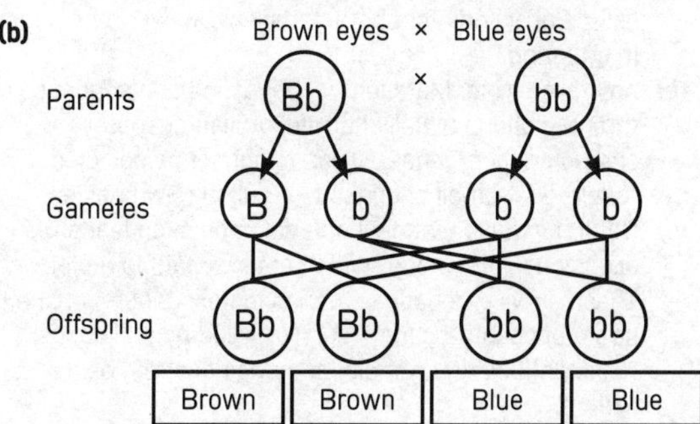

(1 mark will be awarded for each correct row.)

(c) If both parents have heterozygous genes (e.g. Bb) **(1 mark)**; then there is a (one in four) chance of the child having blue eyes **(1 mark)**.

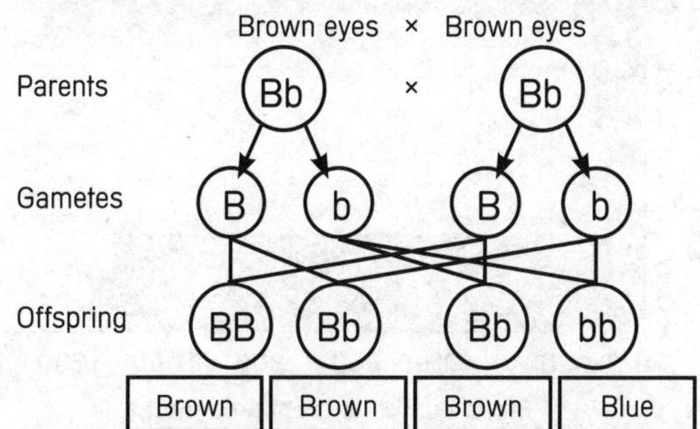

(2 marks for correct diagram.)

6. **(a)**

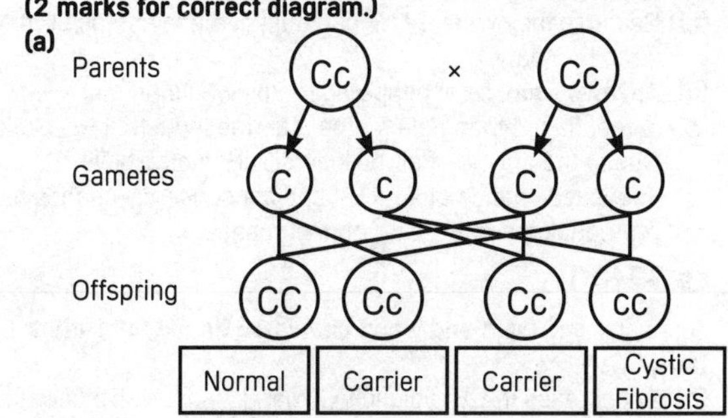

(1 mark will be awarded for each correct row.)

(b) There was a one in four chance/0.25/25%

(c) Heterozygous **should be ringed**.

B2: Understanding Our Environment

Pages 20–21

1. annelids; molluscs; crustaceans; arachnids **should be ringed. (Four correct = 3 marks, three correct = 2 marks, two correct = 1 mark, zero or one correct = 0 marks.)**
2. **(a)** They cannot produce fertile offspring.
   (b) **(i)** **Underline any one of the following**; 'carnivorous big cats'; 'five toes on their front paws and four toes on their back paws'; 'claws can be drawn back'.
   (ii) Leopards are more closely related to tigers **(1 mark)**. Both are the *Panthera* genus/snow leopards are a different genus **(1 mark)**.
3. **(a)** Possesses features which are found in reptiles and birds, e.g. feathers place it with birds but it also has teeth like reptiles; It is an intermediate form.
   (b) **Any two from**: Bacteria reproduce asexually; Therefore difficult to apply concept of 'fertile' offspring; Observable features may often be identical, have to use special stains as a classification tool.
   (c) Similar organisms have similar DNA sequencing; Scientists can look for a close match of DNA to work out relatedness of different groups/species/strains.

Pages 22–23

1. Transfer of energy **should be ticked**.
2. **(a)** A producer is an organism which produces its own food.
   (b) Sunlight/the sun
   (c) **Any one of**: Wasp; Ladybird; Hoverfly
   (d) Diagram **B**
   (e) **Any two from**: Respiration; Reproduction; Egestion (faeces); Movement/muscle contraction in animals; Maintaining body temperature.
3. **(a)** **Any one of**: Plant material; Grass; Cereal crops; Sileage.
   (b) Movement **and** respiration
   (c) 6000 – (2000 + 3000) = 6000 – 5000 = 1000 kJ
4. **(a)** $\frac{1000}{6000} \times 100 = 17\%$ **(1 mark for correct answer, 1 mark for showing working.)**
   (b) Cellulose in plant material requires more energy to digest **(1 mark)**; therefore larger amounts need to be consumed **(1 mark). Accept converse argument for humans.**
   (c) **This is a model answer, which demonstrates QWC, and would therefore score the full 6 marks**: Shorter food chains are more energy efficient because they have fewer trophic levels. A vegetarian food chain may have only two levels: plants – humans, whereas a meat-eating diet will have three or more. We know that energy is lost at each consumer trophic level as respiration, heat, excretion, egestion and movement. In this way, a consumer may lose up to 90% energy. Producing food for a vegetarian population requires decreased areas of land because at least one trophic level is removed from the food chain. A field of wheat will support many more humans than a field of cattle. This can be seen in a pyramid of biomass where the width of the human trophic level is greater when humans are a primary consumer compared with when they are a secondary or tertiary consumer.

Pages 24–25

1. **(a)** Respiration
   (b) **Any two from**: Fossil fuels represent a carbon 'sink'/They absorbed great quantities of carbon dioxide many millions of years ago; Combustion in power stations returns this carbon dioxide to the atmosphere; Less burning of fossil fuels cuts down on carbon emissions; Alternative sources of energy may not return as much carbon dioxide to the atmosphere.
2. **(a)** Nitrogen is too unreactive to be incorporated directly into an animal's body. Animals do not possess the necessary enzymes/adaptations to do this.
   (b) **A** = 1, **B** = 3, **C** = 4, **D** = 2 **(All four correct = 2 marks. Subtract 1 mark for every incorrect answer.)**

3. (a) Peat contains fossilised remains of plants **(1 mark)**; which originally absorbed carbon dioxide from the atmosphere via photosynthesis **(1 mark)**.
   (b) **Any two of**: Eruption of volcanoes adjacent to limestone deposits; Acid rain; Chemical weathering of limestone.
4. (a) Nitrogen-fixing bacteria
   (b) They convert nitrogen to nitrates **(1 mark)**, which can be absorbed by plants **(1 mark)**.
   (c) Nitrates
   (d) Clover has nitrate in its roots, formed by a mutualistic relationship with bacteria **(1 mark)**, so clover ploughed back into the soil fertilises it **(1 mark)**.

Pages 26–27

1. (a)

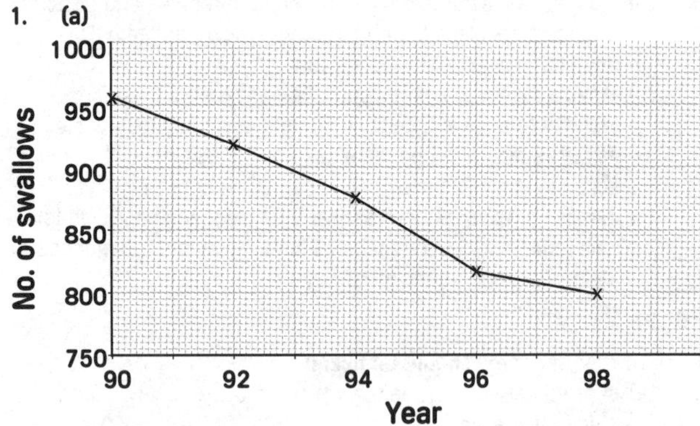

(2 marks for correct plotting, 1 mark for accurate joining of points.)

   (b) 775 (+ 1 − 10)
   (c) Flying insects are prey for swallows **(1 mark)**; so if there are fewer insects there is less food for swallows **(1 mark)**.
2. (a)

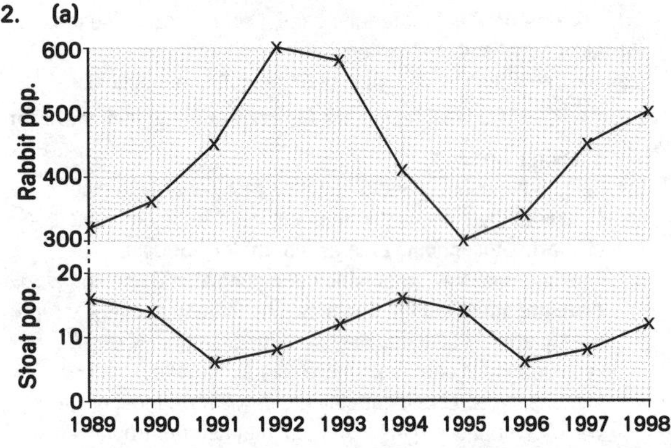

(2 marks for correct plotting, 1 mark for joining of points.)

   (b) As the rabbit population decreases, there is less food (the rabbits) available for the stoats **(1 mark)**; so the stoat population decreases **(1 mark)**; fewer rabbits are eaten, so the rabbit population increases **(1 mark)**.
3. (a) Bacteria convert nitrogen from the air into nitrates. Leguminous plants absorb nitrates and use them to make plant proteins; Pea plants are therefore able to survive in poor soils with low nitrate levels because of these bacteria.
   (b) Plants make sugars by photosynthesis which bacteria absorb and use for respiration to get energy.
4. (a) Niche is the role or 'job description' which an organism carries out in its habitat.
   (b) When two types of ladybird occupy the same niche they compete for the same resources; The native ladybirds are at a competitive disadvantage so are likely to decline in number.

Pages 28–29

1. (a) features; characteristics; suited; environment; evolutionary; survival. **(six words correct = 3 marks, four or five words correct = 2 marks, two or three words correct = 1 mark, one or 0 words correct = 0 marks).**
   (b) **Any two from**: Small ears, reducing heat loss; Insulating fat/ blubber; Thick insulating fur; Fur on soles of feet for insulation; Powerful legs for chasing prey; Sharp claws and teeth for shearing flesh.
   (c) **Any two from**: Eyes at side of head for a wide field of vision; Well-camouflaged; Built for speed/muscular legs for fast running.
2. (a)

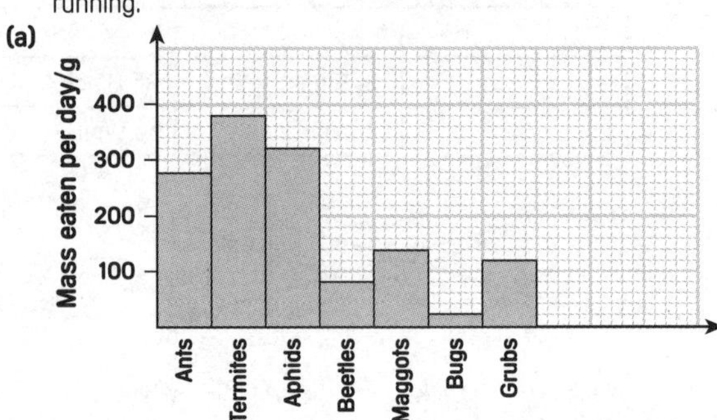

(2 marks for correct plotting of bars, 1 mark for correct labeling of x and y axes.)

   (b) $\frac{380}{1330}$ = 28.6% **(1 mark for correct answer, 1 mark for showing working.)**
   (c) Batink occupies more than one habitat/niche; Eats a wide variety of food/prey.

Pages 30–31

1. evolved, slow; adapted; genes. **(Four words correct = 2 marks, two or three words correct = 1 mark, one or zero words correct = 0 marks.)**
2. (a) **Any one of**: Discovery of DNA/genes/units of inheritance in cells; Carry code for characteristics; Shown to be passed on to offspring.
   (b) **Any three from**: Mutations/changes in base sequence are rare; Mutations usually harmful; Advantageous characteristics/genes/alleles might not be selected for; Time required for small changes to result in new species.
   (c) Natural variation within bacterial population leads to occasional 'mutations', which are resistant to antibiotics; These survive to pass on genes to next generation, natural strain of bacteria cannot survive/killed by antibiotics; Resistant bacteria remain, and original strain becomes extinct.
3. (a) **Pre-Industrial Revolution**; Pale: 1260; Dark: 107 **(1 mark)**. **Post-Industrial Revolution**; Pale: 89; Dark: 1130 **(1 mark)**.
   (b)

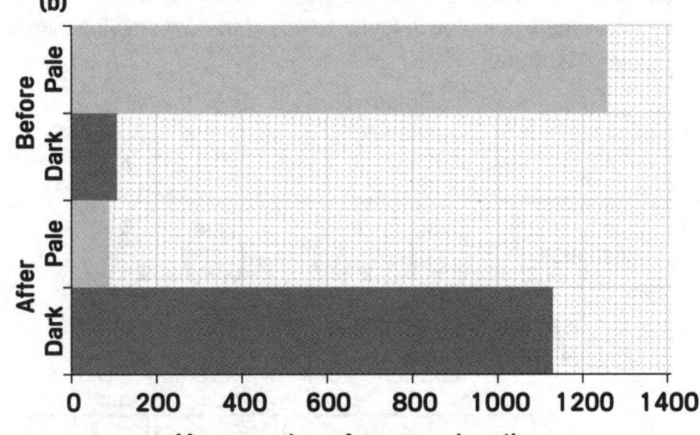

(2 marks for correct plotting of bars.)

   (c) Because they were better camouflaged against the silver birch tree bark.
   (d) **Any two from**: Dark peppered moths would be more camouflaged than pale moths after the Industrial Revolution; Due to the effects of air pollution; Dark moths have increased chance of survival and consequently chance of reproducing and passing on their genes.

Pages 32–33

1. sea water **and** wind **and** wood **should be ringed for 1 mark**.
2. (a) CFCs
   (b) An increase in UV radiation **(1 mark)**; causes skin cells to mutate, which causes melanoma/tumours **(1 mark)**.

3. (a) A UV rays from the sun pass through the atmosphere and are absorbed at the surface.
B infrared radiation cannot 'escape' into space/exit prevented by greenhouse gases.
(b) **Climate belts** shift causing ecosystems and habitats to change, organisms are displaced and become extinct.
Sea levels rise causing flooding of coastal regions, islands are inundated and disappear beneath sea level.
Ice caps and glaciers melt and retreat.
4. (a) 18
(b) 5
(c) Yes **(Yes/No answer carries no marks)**: The presence of species which are adapted to polluted environment, e.g. rat-tailed maggot, water louse (low oxygen concentration) pH acidic, nitrate levels high **(2 marks)**. **Or** No **(Yes/No answer carries no marks)**: Species diversity is not too small, mayfly nymphs are present **(2 marks)**.
(d) Indicator species
5. (a) **see graph**
(b) **see graph**

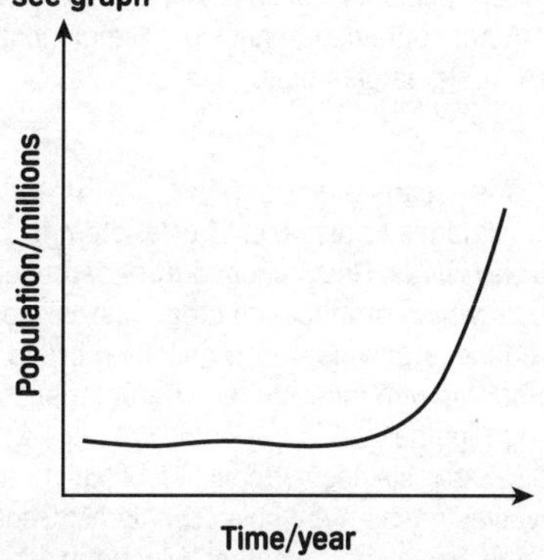

(c) **Any two from**: Insufficient birth control; Better life expectancy; Better health care

Pages 34–35

1. (a) 160 thousand tonnes **(+ 1 – 10 thousand)**
(b) Overall decrease in numbers; Temporary rises in 1978–1983 and 1993–1998.
(c) (i) 1907 tonnes
(ii) **Any two from**: Numbers of haddock still declined; Therefore less fish should be caught; In order for fish stocks to recover.
(d) **Any one of**: Increasing mesh size to allow young cod to reach breeding age; Increase quotas of other fish species.
2. **Any two from**: Climate change; New predators; Habitat destruction; Hunting; Competition; Pollution.
3.

	Advantages	Disadvantages
Breed whales in captivity in zoos	Study whales so that we can protect them more efficiently; **or** Possibly return whales born in captivity to natural environment.	Captive whale behaviour is not the same as that of free whales; **or** Poor survival rate of released whales.
Protect natural habitat	Enable whales to live and reproduce in own environment.	Difficult to prevent pollution, fishing, etc. in open sea.
Make whale hunting illegal	Protect whales from culling. Fewer whales die.	Difficult to enforce laws; **or** Some countries feel it is right to hunt whales.

4. (a) Tourism and hunting businesses might suffer if rhinos are protected.
(b) Maintaining the habitat for grouse shooting is prevented, local economy affected, livelihoods of gamekeepers, etc.
(c) Prevents farmers enlarging fields and maximising profit on crops, hedges hinder movement of large agricultural machines.

B3: Living and Growing

Page 36

1. (a) **Any two from**: Mitochondria are the sites of (aerobic) respiration; Required for release of energy; Muscles need a large amount of energy.
(b) **Correct order**: cell, nucleus, chromosome, gene, base.
2. (a) X – (Nitrogenous) base **(simply writing the letters A, C, T, G will not be enough to gain the mark)**.
(b) Double helix
3. (a) C; T; T; A; G; A; T; G; T **(All correct for 1 mark.)**
(b) 3
(c) 3

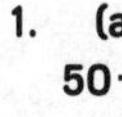

Pages 37–38

1. (a)

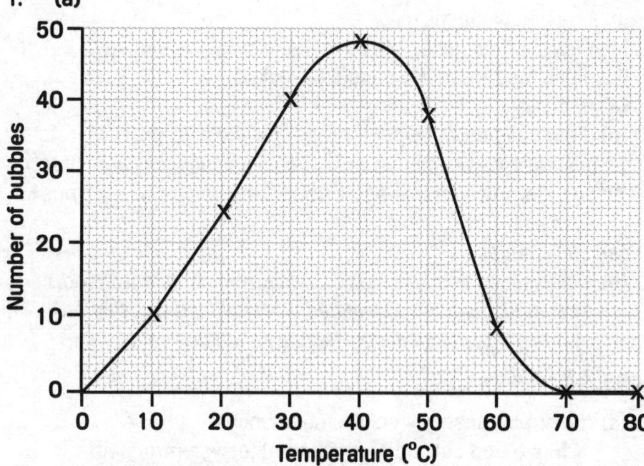

(2 marks for correct plotting, subtract 1 mark for every incorrect plot, 1 mark for smooth curve.)
(b) The rate of bubbles produced increases until it reaches an optimum/maximum; Then it decreases rapidly, reaching no bubbles at 70°C.
(c) 40°C
(d) Acid affects shape of enzyme/active site, substrate no longer fits **(1 mark)**; unable to carry out its function **(1 mark)**.
2. (a) **Any two from**: UV light; Radioactive substances; X-rays; Certain chemicals/mutagens.
(b) **Base/codon/triplet** sequence changed **(1 mark)**, leads to change in **amino acid** sequence **(1 mark) (words in answer in bold must be present to gain marks)**.
3. (a) Denaturation
(b) **Diagram to show**: Change in shape of active site; Substrate no longer fitting active site.
4. At lower temperatures the particles/molecules are not moving as quickly/have less kinetic energy **(1 mark)**, therefore fewer collisions/less molecules collide with sufficient energy **(1 mark)**.

Pages 39–40

1. (a) **Any two from:** Lactic acid increase; In muscles; Causes muscle fatigue/tiredness; Lactic acid is toxic.
(b) Anaerobic respiration releases lower amounts of energy than aerobic, not enough energy available for intense activity.
(c) (i) Aerobic
(ii) Glucose is completely broken down (to carbon dioxide and water).
2. (a) **Any two from**: Transport of substances; Muscle contraction; Nervous conduction; Making new molecules; Maintaining constant body temperature.
(b) Moving blood delivers oxygen to muscles; Removes carbon dioxide (to lungs).
3. $C_6H_{12}O_6 + 6O_2 \longrightarrow 6CO_2 + 6H_2O$
(1 mark for correct reactants, 1 mark for correct products.)
4. (a) The scrubber removes carbon dioxide so that only oxygen consumption is measured; This avoids an inaccurate result.
(b) Larger athletes will use more oxygen due to their higher muscle mass; The adjustment allows rates to be fairly/accurately compared.

(c) Boris' consumption rate would be lower; This is because his lungs, heart, and muscles are less efficient at transporting/using oxygen.
(d) Sprinting has a greater energy demand **(1 mark)**; therefore more oxygen is needed **(1 mark)**.
(e) The higher temperature would raise consumption level **(1 mark)**; because increased temperature increases the enzyme activity in Isaac's muscles **(1 mark)**.

Pages 41–42

1. Specialised organs carry out a specific job, multi-cellular organisms are complex and require specialised organs so they can grow larger; Single-celled organisms are small enough not to require specialised cells and transport systems.
2. **Mitosis**: No (little) variation **Meiosis**: Sexual reproduction; Produces cells with 23 chromosomes.
3. gametes; haploid; meiosis.
4. Meiosis shuffles genes which make each gamete unique; Gametes fuse randomly **should be ticked**.
5. **(a)** Meiosis
   (b) Four cells produced (in second meiotic division).
6. **1st box**: New bases pair up with exposed bases on each strand.
   2nd box: Cells divide/split apart, copies move to opposite ends/poles of cell.
7. **(a)** Differentiation
   (b) Specialised tissue/transport system needed to transport materials over long distances; Paramecium can rely on diffusion due to larger surface area/volume ratio.

Pages 43–44

1. **(a)** **Plasma**: transports soluble substances.
   White blood cell: part of the immune system/engulf microbes or pathogens/produces antibodies.
   Red blood cell: transports oxygen.
   Platelet: involved in clotting process/repair of damaged blood.
   (Four correct = 3 marks, three correct = 2 marks, two correct = 1 mark, zero or one correct = 0 marks.)
   (b) Lungs

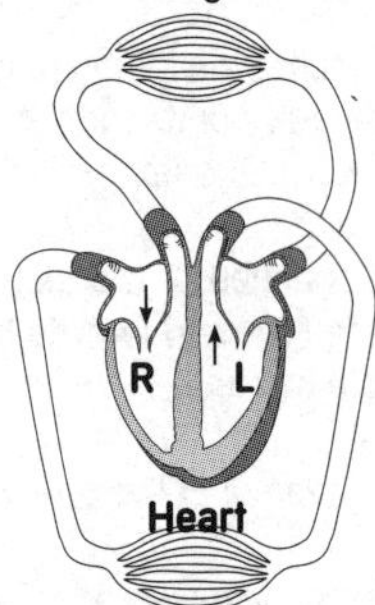

Body

   (c) Blood vessels **i** and **iv should be ringed.**
   (d) Left ventricle has to pump blood over a much longer distance covering most body organs. Right ventricle only has to pump blood to lungs and back.
2. 50 mm ÷ 40 = 0.125 cm/1.25 mm **(1 mark for correct answer, 1 mark for showing working)**.
3. **(a)** **A** – Artery; **B** – Vein.
   (b) Artery has to withstand/recoil with higher pressure, elasticity allows smoother blood flow/second boost to blood when recoils.
   (c) Vein has valves to prevent backflow of blood/compensate for low blood pressure.
4. Results in higher overall blood pressure/greater flow rate.
5. haemoglobin + oxygen $\rightleftharpoons$ oxyhaemoglobin

Pages 45–46

1. **A** – 3; **B** – 2; **C** – 1
2. **(a)** Undifferentiated animal cells **(1 mark)**; can specialise into a whole range of cells, tissues or organs **(1 mark)**.
   (b) **Any two from**: Cancer research; Drug testing; Transplants (which will not be rejected).
3. **(a)** Exponential phase
   (b) Growth is minimal/no more growth
   (c) S or sigma-shaped curve (also called a sigmoid curve).
4. **(a)** **(i)** 12
   (ii) 14
   (b) Boys go through puberty later than girls.
5. **This is a model answer, which demonstrates QWC, and would therefore score the full 6 marks**: Stem cells are useful for research because they are undifferentiated and therefore can become any type of cell. This is especially true of embryonic stem cells. Scientists can use these cells to investigate how cell division can go wrong and cause diseases such as cancer. They can also activate stem cell genes to become particular tissues or even organs, which have potential use in transplant surgery. Embryonic stem cells tend to come from IVF treatment where excess cells not used in the treatment of infertile couples are preserved. This produces an ethical conflict for some people as these embryos have the potential to become a human being and yet are discarded after 14 days (currently in the UK). Embryonic stem cells are difficult to control and it may take many attempts before scientists can obtain a particular cell line. There is also a risk of an immune reaction as stem cells from a random embryo donor are more likely to face rejection after transplantation.
6. **Any two from**: DNA not contained in nucleus; Simple loop of DNA; Source DNA exists as plasmids.

Pages 47–48

1. **(a)** More seed heads; Heads are larger.
   (b) **Any one of**: Resistance to disease; Shorter stem to withstand strong winds; Resistance to frost damage.
2. **(a)** Select the cows which produce the creamiest milk and the cows that produce large volumes of milk then breed them; Select the offspring with the required characteristics; Breed these offspring together.
   (b) **Any one of**: Disease resistance; Production of high quality beef.
3. **Any two from**: Involves genes not whole organisms; Genes transferred from one organism to another; Much more precise in terms of passing on characteristics; Rapid production; Cheaper than selective breeding.
4. **(a)** Crops containing soya can be sprayed with herbicide so weeds killed rather than soya.
   (b) Rice produces carotene, nourishes poor populations with added vitamin A.
5. No, scientists should not continue with their research because: **Any three from**: GM plants may cross-breed with wild plants and release new genes into the environment; Parents may want to modify their children's characteristics; Foetus' screening may lead to 'undesirable foetus' being aborted; There may be unknown safety issues with GM foods; Reduction in human gene pool.
   OR
   Yes, scientists should continue their research because: GM allows the development of new genetic combinations to replace faulty genes, e.g. cystic fibrosis; GM plants can be manufactured to exhibit greater yields, disease resistance, greater nutritional content etc; GM can be used to grow transplant organs which will not be rejected **(these are just some of the applications)**.
6. **(a)** **Step 3** – Section of human DNA inserted into plasmid by enzyme.
   Step 5 – Bacterium replicates/cultivated in fermenter.
   (b) Restriction enzyme

Pages 49–50

1. **(a)** Mitosis
   (b) It enables them to produce many plants with the desired characteristics from just one parent plant.
   (c) If plants are susceptible to a disease or change, all the plants with those genes will be affected; Reduction in genetic variation reduces potential for further selective breeding.
2. **(a)** The organ might be rejected by the recipient's immune system.
   (b) **(i)** The process can be used to generate stem cells for research.
   (ii) The possibility of producing multiple adult clones artificially raises the problem of human rights for the same individuals.
3. **Stage 1** – Select a parent with desired characteristics.
   Stage 2 – Scrape off a large number of small tissue pieces.
   Stage 3 – Grow plants in sterile medium and repeat process.

4. **Benefits, any two from**: Same characteristics in all cloned animals; Sex and timing of birth can be chosen; Top quality bulls and cows can be kept for sperm and egg donation.
   Risks, any two from: Cloning reduces herd's genetic variation; Animals can become in-bred; Cloned animals might not live as long as 'normal' animals.

B4: It's a Green World

Pages 51–52

1. **(a)** Habitat
   (b) Ecosystem
   (c) **Any one of**: Pooter; Sweepnet; Light trap.
   (d) **(i)** 16 x 4 x 5000 = 320,000 **(1 mark for correct answer, 1 mark for showing working.)**
   (ii) **Any one of**: Not enough quadrats laid; Quadrats not distributed throughout the meadow.
   (e) **(i)** Beetles compete, for same resources; Numbers reduce as resources are limited.
   (ii) Snail numbers would decline.
2. **(a)** 79 (rounded-up, working: (15 × 21) ÷ 4) **(1 mark for correct answer, 1 mark for showing working.)**
   (b) **Any two from**: No immigration/emigration; Marking animals does not affect their distribution; Animals are evenly distributed; Animals do not become 'trap happy'.
   (c) Even/wider distribution of traps around field; Use more traps.

Pages 53–54

1. **(a)** Leaves
   (b) **Cellulose**: Cell wall; **Protein Any one of**: Growth; Repair; Enzyme production.
2. carbon dioxide + water ⟶ glucose + oxygen
   (1 mark for reactants, 1 mark for products.)
3. **(a)** An increased temperature and an increased carbon dioxide concentration **(1 mark)**, increases rate of photosynthesis, therefore increases starch production/yield **(1 mark)**.
   (b) Increase light regime, e.g. artificial lighting switched on at night time.
4. **(a)** 3600 **(2 marks for correct answer, but if incorrect, 30 × 120 would gain 1 mark.)**
   (b) Carbon dioxide is also incorporated from the atmosphere.
   (c) Mineral ions/nutrients
   (d) Minerals absorbed in small amounts.
5. **(a)**

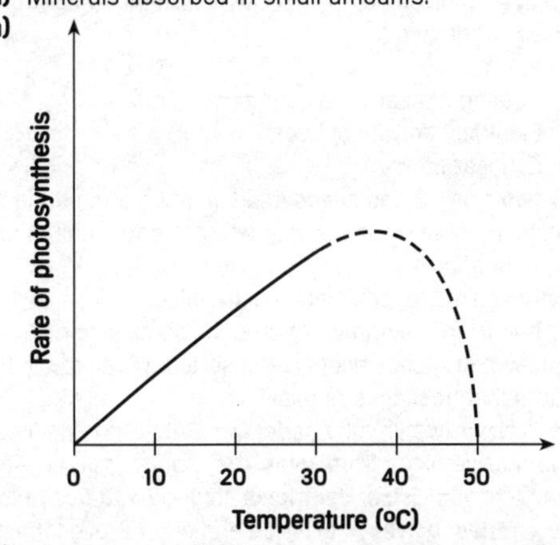

   (b) As the temperature increases, the rate increases due to more rapid molecular movement; By 40°C, the rate peaks and beyond this the enzyme becomes denatured and the reaction stops.
6. **(a)** X
   (b) **D** should be marked above B on x-axis. **N** should be marked above E on x-axis.

Page 55

1. **From top**: (Upper) Epidermis: Spongy layer/mesophyll; Air space.
2. **(a)** Raw material for photosynthesis; Required to transport materials, evaporation from leaf cools plant.
   (b) **Any three from**: Water evaporates from mesophyll cell surface; Resulting in a high concentration of water vapour; In the air spaces of the leaf; Water moves by diffusion, through the stomata to the atmosphere.
3. **Upper epidermis**: Is transparent; To allow transmission of light to palisade layer.
   Palisade cells: Positioned near top of leaf for maximum absorption of light/packed with chloroplasts; Chloroplasts are mobile for maximum absorption of light.
   Spongy mesophyll: Has many air spaces; For rapid diffusion of gases/carbon dioxide.

Pages 56–57

1. **(a)** **Any two named small nutrient molecules**, e.g. glucose, vitamins, minerals, ions, amino acids, oxygen.
   (b) **Any one of**: Carbon dioxide; Urea.
2. **Any two from**: Water moves down concentration gradient/from high water concentration to low water concentration; Across a partially/differentially permeable membrane/plasma membrane; Gradient maintained by input and output of water at each end of cell line.
3. Water moving from plant cell to plant cell; A pear losing water in a concentrated solution; Water moving from blood plasma to body cells **should be ticked. (Subtract 1 mark for any additional ticks.)**
4. **(a)** Sugar molecules are too large to pass through.
   (b)

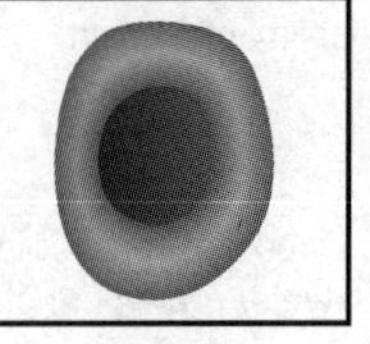
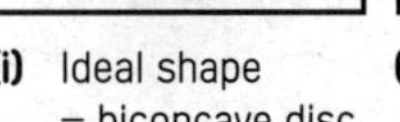
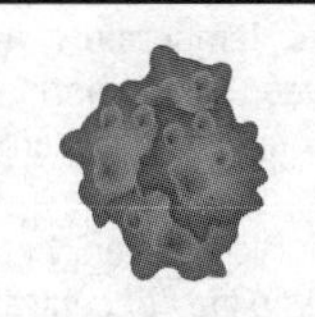
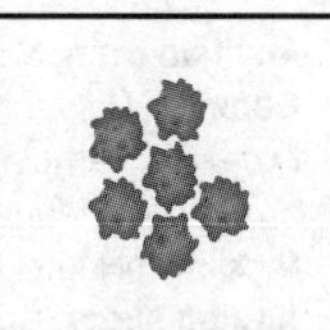

(i) Ideal shape – biconcave disc
(ii) Cell crenated (appearance looks shrivelled)
(iii) Cell bursts (cell not visible/ fragments remain)

5. **(a)** **Any two from**: Cells swell/turgid; Due to influx of water; By osmosis.
   (b) **Any two from**: Cells shrink; Cytoplasm pulls away from wall; Cells plasmolysed; Vacuole shrinks.
   (c) It would droop.
   (d) **Any two from**: Water drawn out of plant/roots; By osmosis; Cells no longer turgid; Flaccid cells cannot support plant effectively.

Pages 58–59

1. **(a)** **Roots**: anchor plant in soil/absorb water and minerals.
   Stem: supports leaves and flowers, transports substances to leaves.
   Leaves: organs of photosynthesis.
   Flowers: reproductive organs, formation of seeds.
   (b) **(i)** Phloem
   (ii) Xylem
2. **(a)** Ensure no water evaporated into the air.
   (b) $\frac{(50-40)}{4} = 2.5$ **(1 mark for correct answer, 1 mark for showing working.)**
   (c) Volume decreased **(1 mark)**; due to uptake by plant **(1 mark)**.
   (d) **(i)** Less water uptake by plant.
   (ii) Less water uptake by plant.
   (iii) Increased air movement results in more water uptake.
3. **Any two from**: Dead cells without cytoplasm; No end walls; Hollow lumen; Continuous tubes – all adaptations allow efficient movement of water in columns.
4. **This is a model answer, which demonstrates QWC, and would therefore score the full 6 marks**: As light intensity increases during the day, the rate of photosynthesis increases in the guard cells. This results in more sugar being manufactured, which raises the solute concentration. The guard cells will therefore draw in water from surrounding cells by osmosis, thus becoming more turgid. This causes the stoma to become wider. The arrangement of cellulose in the cell walls of the guard cells means that there is differential expansion in the outer wall resulting in an increasing aperture of the stoma.

Page 60

1. (a)

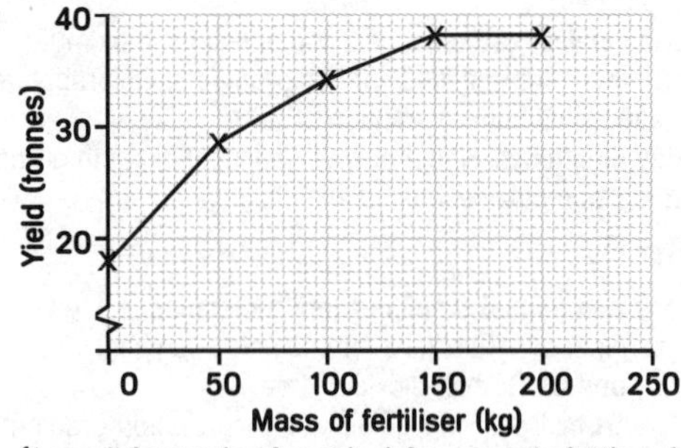

(1 mark for scale of graph, 1 for correct plotting, 1 for correct line.)

(b) The size of each field; The number of barley seeds planted in each field.

(c) The first field (where no fertiliser was added).

2. (a) Root hair cells

(b) **Any two from**: Minerals absorbed using release of energy from respiration; Against a concentration gradient; By active transport.

Pages 61–62

1. **Any two from**: Moisture; Temperature; Availability of oxygen.
2. **Canning**: Prevents oxygen from entering.
   Freezing: Temperature too low for microbes to reproduce/ enzymes to work.
   Pickling: pH too low for microbes/enzymes to work, microbes killed.
   Adding sugar: Conditions too concentrated, water drawn out of microbes by osmosis.
3. (a) Flask **B**
   (b) Air/oxygen is able to enter and provide conditions for decay in **B** and microbes can enter.
   (c) To kill microbes/Drive out air/oxygen.
4. (a) **Any two from:** Earthworms; Maggots; Woodlice.
   (b) They break down detritus into smaller particles over a larger surface area **(1 mark)**; making it easier for decomposers to feed on **(1 mark)**.
5. **Any two from**: Sewage treatment; Compost heaps; Biogas.
6. (a) Saprophytes feed on dead/decaying material, secrete enzymes externally on to food **(1 mark)**; absorb digested products, extra-cellular digestion **(1 mark)**.
   (b) As water content increases the dry mass of toadstools also increases; Difference in rate of dry mass increase not as great at higher moisture levels.
   (c) YES: Produces greatest increase in toadstool dry mass. **OR** NO: No data for moisture greater than 30 g/100 ml, might produce greater increases in toadstool dry mass.
   (d) Water content of toadstools might vary considerably according to other factors **(1 mark)**; leading to inaccurate results/experiment being invalid **(1 mark)**.

Pages 63–64

1. (a) Chemicals used to kill pests.
   (b) Chemicals which kill weeds (and therefore reduce the energy taken in by these competitors).
   (c) (i) Weeding by hand.
   (ii) By using biological control.
   (d) **Any two from**: Using compost/manure; Crop rotation; Leguminous plants.
2. (a) (i) So the cows do not have to waste valuable energy keeping themselves warm; The energy can be used for new growth.
   (ii) So the cows do not waste energy in movement.
   (b) **Any one of**: Easy to control what they eat; Easy to feed/milk; Animals do not stray.
   (c) Diseases spread quickly.
   (d) **Any one of**: They have a lower quality of life; The animals are more stressed.
3. (a) Growing plants without soil.
   (b) Excessive use of inorganic fertilisers/chemicals
   (c) **Temperature**: use heaters
   Light: use lamps
   Carbon dioxide: use wood burning stove/equivalent
4. **Advantage, any one of**: Minerals can be carefully adjusted; Reduced risk of plants becoming diseased.
   Disadvantage: Plants have to be supported due to lack of anchorage.
5. Pesticides flow into rivers where they are absorbed by algae; The algae is eaten by zooplankton; The pesticide is persistent/ is not excreted/not lost from bodies of organisms so the concentration increases as it moves up the food chain until larger organisms/top consumers are harmed.

B5: The Living Body

Pages 65–66

1. **Any two from**: Provides a shape/framework for the body; Grows with the body; Easy to attach muscles to.
2. **The correct words, in order, are**: earthworm; external; chitin; cartilage. **(All correct for 2 marks; 2 correct for 1 mark)**
3. (a) (i) (Head of) bone (ii) Hollow shaft/bone marrow and blood vessels (iii) Cartilage.
   (b) Bone would pierce skin and muscle.
   (c) Tendons attach muscles to bones; And therefore allow the fingers to move/damaged tendons mean that fingers won't move effectively.
4. It makes them stronger **(1 mark)** and lighter **(1 mark)**.
5. (a) Hinge
   (b) **B**
   (c) **X** relaxed; **Y** contracted
   (d) Muscle antagonism
6. Muscles attached close to fulcrum **(1 mark)** allows greater range of movement for a given force **(1 mark)**.
7. (a) Ossification
   (b) Cartilage replaced **(1 mark)**; by calcium and phosphorus salts **(1 mark)**.
   (c) Proportion of cartilage to bone measured **(1 mark)**; comparing measurements at different ages gives indication that growth is occurring **(1 mark)**.

Pages 67–68

1. (a) **Locust: Any two from**: Blood not contained in vessels; Slow circulation; Does not deliver oxygen to tissues; Blood pumped by action of muscles attached to skeleton.
   (b) **Deer**: Blood pumped by a heart; Flows in blood vessels.
2. (a) Two fingers placed on neck or wrist; Count number of pulses in one minute.
   (b) (i) Aorta
   (ii) Beating of heart/contacting of ventricles
   (c) (i) Electrical activity of heart
   (ii) Echocardiogram
   (d) **Any two from**: Blood needs to be pumped around the body faster; To deliver more oxygen and glucose to the muscles; For respiration.
3. (a) Rhythmically produce electrical impulses.
   (b) **Any two from**: Rhythmically produce small electrical impulses; Artificial pacemaker inserted; Wired to the heart to ensure that beating is regular.
4. (a) **P** = AVN/Atrioventricular node; **Q** = SAN/Sinoatrial node
   (b) **Atria** receive blood from **veins**, they contract and push blood down into **ventricles**; **Ventricles** contract and push blood up into **arteries**; **Valves** in **arteries** and heart prevent backflow of blood.
5. **Galen** believed that blood flowed like a tide between the liver and the heart.
   Harvey showed that the heart pumped blood through vessels, arteries carried blood away from the heart, and valves in veins prevented backflow.

Pages 69–70

1. (a) **Any one from**: To prevent excess blood loss; **or** Prevent pathogens/microbes from entering the bloodstream.
   (b) Vitamin K **and** vitamin C.
   (c) Break down the clot.
   (d) (i) 100 seconds **(2 marks), but if the answer is incorrect then showing the working,** $\frac{(101 + 99)}{2}$**, will gain 1 mark.**
   (ii) Rats have different body masses/to standardise results.

(iii) As warfarin dose increases the time to clot also increases.
(iv) **Any one of**: Need more data/more samples; Rats could be different ages/varieties; Higher or lower doses not tested.

2. **(a)** **Any one of**: Blood/plasma transfusion; Transfusion of factor 8; Platelets transferred.
(b) **Any one of**: HIV infection; Hepatitis B infection; Raised white cell count; Anaemia, etc.
(c) Blood cells would be agglutinated/clumped by the recipient's antibodies.
(d) **Any one of**: Religious objections; Fear of blood-borne disease, e.g. HIV and Hep B.
3. **(a)** Anti-A and Anti-B
(b) O
(c) Platelets/blood exposed to air; A series of chemical reactions follow resulting in a mesh of fibrin forming.
4. **(a)** The placenta/the mother's blood supply
(b) Oxygenated and deoxygenated blood mixing
(c) Operation to close hole in heart

Pages 71–72

1. **(a)** Total volume of air available for gas exchange in the lungs.
(b) Agree: Because as vital capacity increased the time underwater also increased.
Or disagree, **any one of**: Only five subjects/not enough data; Need to find divers with higher/lower vital capacities.
(c) **Breathing** is the process whereby air enters the lungs. **Respiration** is energy release in cells.
(d) **Any two from**: Test a wider range of subjects; Need to take account of gender of diver; Standardise ages; Standardise fitness levels.
(e) (i)

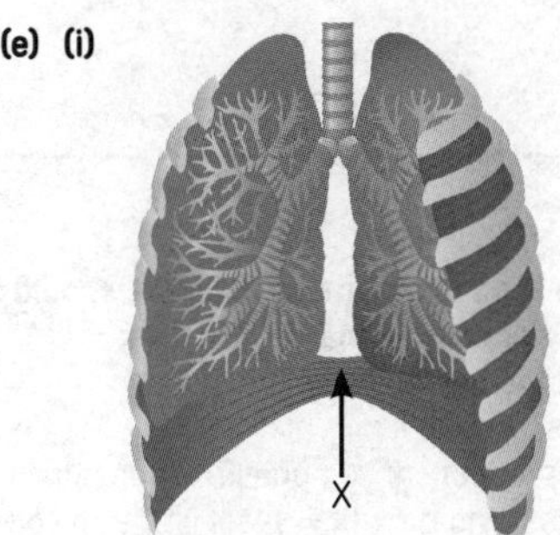

(ii) **Any two from**: Diaphragm contracts and flattens; Increases chest volume; Chest pressure drops; Air forced in from atmosphere due to difference in pressure.
(f) Tidal volume = 1 litre
2. Mucus traps foreign particles; Beating cilia sweep contaminated mucus up trachea.
3. Airways narrow and muscles around them tighten. Increased production of sticky phlegm **(1 mark)**. Symptoms, **any two of**: Wheezing; Coughing; Chest tightness.

Page 73

1. **(a)**

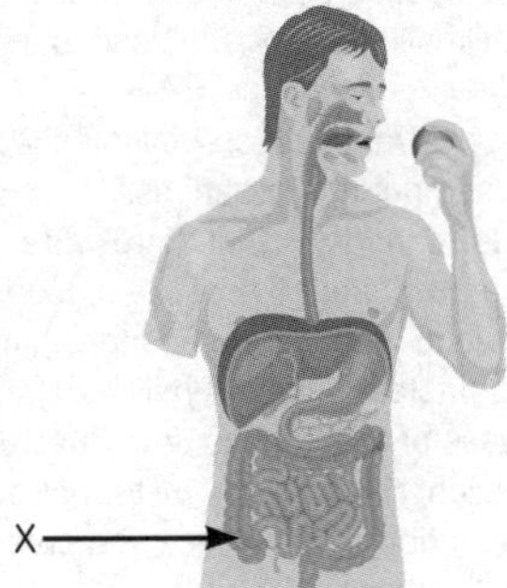

(b)

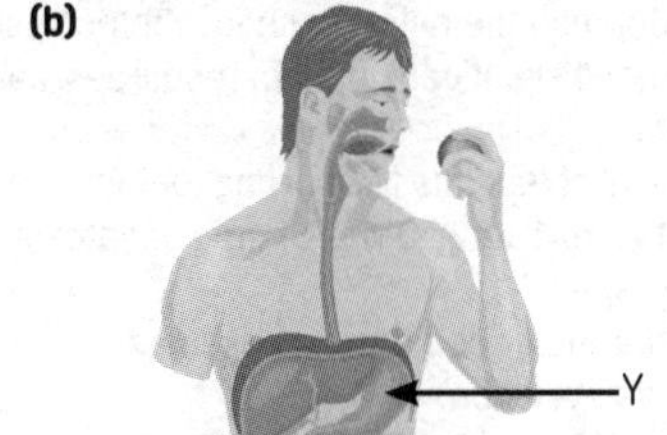

(c) **Symptom** – diarrhoea; **Reason**: Water not absorbed, leading to watery faeces.
2. **This is a model answer, which demonstrates QWC, and would therefore score the full 6 marks**: The small intestine is very long, which allows maximum opportunity for food molecules to be absorbed. The presence of villi increases the surface area for absorption of food molecules. The lining of the intestine is very thin and therefore shortens the diffusion distance and aids rapid diffusion of soluble products. There is an extensive capillary network, which receives the dissolved food products. The villi themselves move around, bringing them into constant contact with higher concentrations of dissolved food substances in the lumen. The peristaltic movements of the small intestine and removal of absorbed products in the capillaries maintains the diffusion gradient, which facilitates further absorption.

Pages 74–75

1. **(a)** Releases (more) sweat; Evaporates, taking heat from skin.
(b) Excretion
(c) Amino acids
(d) **1st box**: Urea enters/is carried in blood; **2nd box**: Urine stored in bladder.
(e) (i) A
(ii) B
(iii) C
(iv) **Any three from**: Low water level in blood detected by receptors/in blood vessels/in brain; More ADH released by pituitary gland; Acts on collecting duct/kidney; Which is stimulated to absorb more water back into bloodstream.
2. **(a)** **Any one of**: Sodium; Chloride; Glucose; Salt; Amino acids; Fatty acids; Glycerol, etc.
(b) **Any three from**: Equal concentrations of useful materials in blood and dialysis fluid; Membrane is selectively permeable; Urea moves down concentration gradient; Into dialysis fluid.

Pages 76–77

1. **Any two from**: Blocked fallopian tubes; Insufficient sperm produced; Sperm not active/mobile; Inability to produce eggs/eggs don't mature.
2. Days 5–14: Uterus wall is being repaired; Egg released at approx. 14 days; Days 14–28 uterus lining maintained.
3. **(a)** Fertilisation outside of the body/'in glass'.
(b) (i) Hormone/FSH
(ii) Many embryos are implanted to ensure that at least one is successful. This can lead to multiple births, which can carry health risks.
(c) **Artificial insemination**: Sperm from father put directly into the uterus.
Egg donation: Eggs from another female are fertilised by IVF and then transplanted.
Surrogacy: Embryo produced by IVF and implanted into the uterus of another woman.
4. **(a)** Hypodermic needle enters uterus, withdraws amniotic fluid containing foetal cells; Cells checked for genetic abnormalities.

(b) (i) Have an abortion/keep the baby/proceed with normal birth; Child will need significant input of resources/care for the rest of life.
(ii) Any one of: Ethical objections to aborting foetus if an abnormality is found; 1 in 200 risk of amniocentesis causing miscarriage.

5. Hormone (either progesterone or oestrogen); Taken as contraceptive pill prevents ovulation.

Pages 78–79

1. (a) Any two from: Diet; Amount of exercise; Amount of growth hormone produced; General health; Diseases contracted. **(Two answers required for 1 mark.)**
(b) Any two from: Fewer industrial diseases; Better diets; Better healthcare; Better housing conditions.

2. (a) Any one of: Shortage of donors; Requires correct tissue match; Kidney must be correct age/size; Donor must be healthy.
(b) Kidney machine/part is too large/not compact enough.
(c) Relatives must be consulted.

3. (a) To prevent organ rejection.
(b) The drugs reduce a person's ability to fight other infections/make them more vulnerable to new infections.

4. (a) Accept either one of the following or any suitable answer: Shortage of donor organs; Long waiting times.
(b) Might be against religious/cultural beliefs.

5. (a)

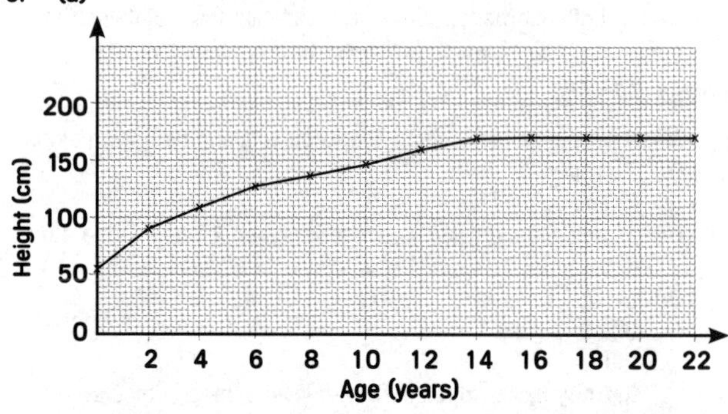

(2 marks for correct plotting (subtract one for every incorrect point), 1 mark for joining points accurately with a line (NOT bars).)
(b) 0 and 2 years
(c) 16 years

6. (a) Any one of: Elderly people suffer from degenerative diseases; They find it increasingly difficult to live in their own homes; May have no one to look after them; Often have to live on a limited income; Hard to maintain a healthy lifestyle.
(b) Burden on economy/taxpayers supporting an expanding elderly population; Burden on NHS.

B6: Beyond the Microscope

Pages 80–81

1. (a) A: Cell wall; **B**: DNA; **C**: Flagellum
(b) C used for movement

2. (a) Any two from: Bleach/disinfect work surface; Wash hands before and after experiment; Sterilise equipment in autoclave; Keep lids on petri dishes; or any other sensible precaution, e.g. no hand-to-mouth operations, cover up cuts, etc.
(b) Any two from: Source of sugar; Warm temp/37°C; Optimum pH; Remove alcohol waste product.
(c) (i) Sketch to show smaller cell 'budding off' a larger one **(1 mark) and** one of the following: Nucleus; Vacuole; Cell wall **(1 mark)**. (Not necessarily labelled.) **(See following diagram.)**
(ii) Mark nucleus with an **X**.

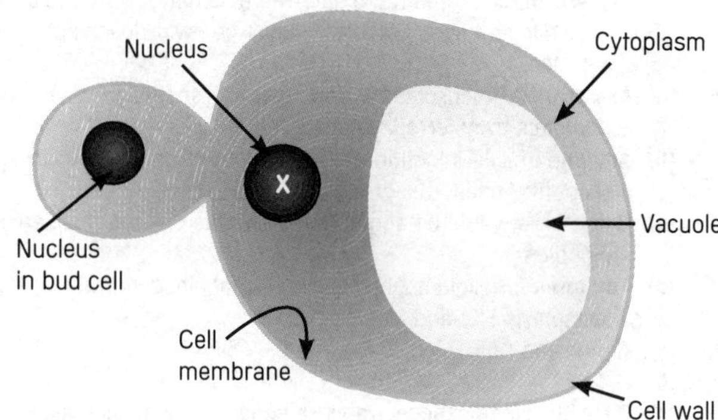

(d) Viruses can only reproduce inside other living cells.

3. Any two from: Consume food sources directly; Photosynthesise; Chemosynthesise.

4. (a)

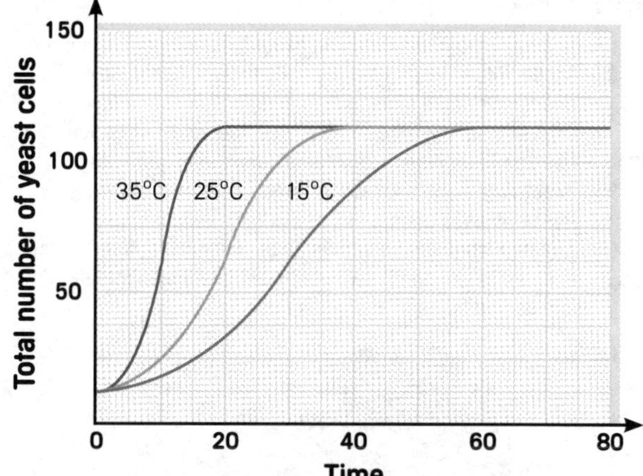

Curve should be to right of other two (1 mark), should level off at same number of cells (1 mark).
(b) Enzymes in yeast cells denatured.
(c) 112–113 yeast cells
(d) Lag phase, slow reproduction; Log phase, exponential growth; Plateau phase, no growth – yeast limited by other factors.

Pages 82–83

1. (a) Pathogen
(b) Any two from: Airborne/through nose/mouth; Contaminated food/water; Injection via insect vectors or hypodermic needles; Sexual contact/exchange of body fluids.

2. (a) Toxin
(b) Any two from: Damaged sewage/water systems; Electricity supplies disrupted/fridges/freezers/cookers don't work; Medical services disrupted; Roads/transport routes disrupted.
(c) Antiseptics can only be applied outside the body.

3. Fleming: Discovered penicillin; Used it as antibiotic to treat bacterial infections.
Lister: Discovered carbolic acid/antiseptic; Prevented wounds from becoming infected. Used during operations.
Pasteur: Responsible for germ theory – that there were microbes in the air, and that they were the cause of food decay; Led to changes in the way food was stored. Responsible for anti-rabies inoculation and pasteurisation of milk.

4. (a) Number of reported cases of MRSA goes down/decreases; Nov 2007–Feb 2008 slight rise followed by further decrease.
(b) Any one of: Over-prescription of antibiotics; Patients not taking full course of antibiotics.
(c) Increased cleanliness/hygiene in hospitals.

Pages 84–85

1. (a) (i) 4; **(ii)** 3; **(iii)** 2; **(iv)** 5; **(v)** 1
(b) Lactobacillus (**allow** Thermophilus)

2. (a) Cider – Apples; Beer – Malted barley; Wine – Grapes.
(b) Sugar/glucose ⟶ ethanol + carbon dioxide

(c) (i) To prevent entry of harmful microbes, to prevent carbon dioxide from escaping.
(ii) To clarify the beer/allow yeast to settle out.
(iii) The beer is pasteurised; The beer is sealed in casks/bottled. **(Both answers needed for 1 mark)**

3. To concentrate the alcohol.
4. To respire/remove the sugar in waste water.
5. Carbon dioxide causes 'fizziness'; Apparatus needs to have a tube/vent to allow carbon dioxide to escape.
6. **(a)** $C_6H_{12}O_6 \longrightarrow 2C_2H_5OH + 2CO_2$ **(1 mark for correct formulae, 1 mark for correct balancing of equation)**
   (b) (Alcohol would not be produced) Only water and carbon dioxide would be produced.
   (c) (i) 30 cm^3
   (ii) 40°C
   (d) It is heated to 72°C **(1 mark)**; then cooled quickly **(1 mark)**.
   (e) To increase the alcohol content of the beer.

Pages 86–87

1. **(a)** Biogas
   (b) Organic material is 'fed' in continuously **(1 mark)**; and biogas is siphoned off regularly **(1 mark)**.
   (c) **Any two from**: Burned to generate electricity; Burned to produce hot water/steam/for central heating; Used as fuel in houses.
   (d) Remote areas don't have access to mains electricity. Burning biogas can generate electricity.
2. **(a)** Petrol/diesel
   (b) Plants grown to make biofuels use up the carbon dioxide made when the biofuel is burned **(1 mark)**; therefore there is no net production of CO_2 **(1 mark)**.
   (c) **Any one of**: Cleaner burning/less particulates; Biofuels are renewable.
3. **(a)** Gas mixture would explode.
   (b) **Any two from**: Fatty acids; Amino acids; Glycerol.
   (c) At low temperatures little biogas is produced/bacteria reproduce/respire slowly; At high temperatures bacterial enzymes are denatured.
4. **This is a model answer, which demonstrates QWC, and would therefore score the full 6 marks**: The advantages of this genetically engineered maize are that less fossil fuels are burned during the processing of maize. The genetic engineering process in laboratories means that production times are reduced and therefore the costs to the manufacturer are less. Transport costs are reduced between production and supply because there is no need to transport costly fossil fuels and the costs of the fermentation process are eliminated as the ethanol is produced *in situ*. The main disadvantage is that the maize might cross-pollinate with other species with detrimental results. For example, wild species of plant may inherit this gene and produce unpredictable effects in the environment, which have 'knock on' effects in the food chain.

Pages 88–89

1. **(a)** detritivore **should be ringed**.
   (b) Burrows mix soil layers; Aerate soil with burrows; Drag organic matter into soil, which then decomposes, neutralises acid soil.
2. Clay – Small mineral particles; Sandy – Large mineral particles; Loam – Mixture of clay and sand.
3. **(a)** 18.9%; $\frac{9.9}{52.3} \times 100$ **(1 mark for correct answer, 1 mark for showing working.)**
   (b) Heat again, re-weigh; Repeat to constant mass
   (c) Dead/decaying plant material
   (d) Burn off humus from dry soil, weigh; Subtract this mass from dry soil mass.
4. Large particle size **(1 mark)**; means large air spaces, which let water through easily **(1 mark)**.
5. **(a)** Centipede
   (b) Herbivore/primary consumer
   (c) Energy and biomass lost at each trophic level **(1 mark)**; due to respiration, egestion/excretion **(1 mark)**, therefore only small proportion passed on to next trophic level **(1 mark)**.
6. **(a)** Plants cannot absorb minerals as well.
   (b) Add lime/alkali

Pages 90–91

1. **(a)** **Any one of**: Less variation in temperature; Support for the organism's body; Easy to dispose of waste products.
   (b) Water more difficult to move over respiratory surface; Therefore making gas exchange less efficient.
   (c) Zooplankton
   (d) (i) **Any four from**: Fertilisers or sewage run-off into waterways; Increases amount of nitrate/phosphate in water; Algal blooms develop/Competitive over other plant life; Blocking off sunlight, leading to the death of other plants; Algae/plants die and decompose; Aerobic bacteria increase as they feed off dead plant material; Oxygen used up in the process; Other organisms unable to respire and therefore die.
   (ii) **Any one of**: Light (intensity); Temperature
   (e) **Any one of**: Household washing up liquid/domestic waste water; Industrial cleaning processes.
   (f) **Organisms used, any two from**: Midge larvae; Stonefly larvae; Damselfly nymphs; Rat-tailed maggot. **(1 mark)**
   Pollutants, any one of: Sewage; Crude oil; PCBs; Pesticides. **(1 mark)**
   Biodiversity: Reduced/lower numbers of different species/only hardy biological indicator species found. **(1 mark)**
2. **(a)** **Any one of**: Krill; Penguin; Seal; Killer whale.
   (b)

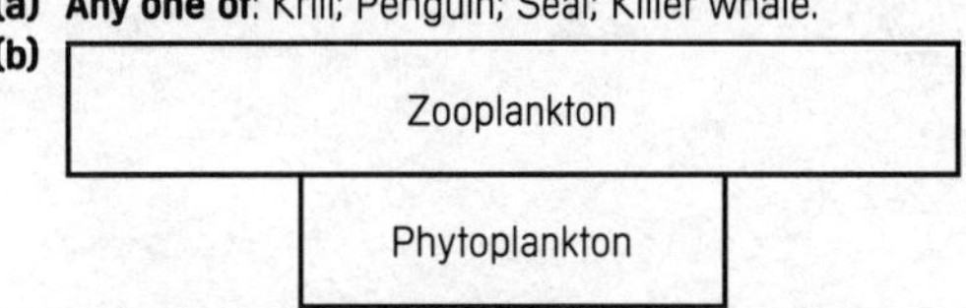

(1 mark for correct trophic level blocks – top wider than bottom, 1 mark for correct labelling.)

3. Continuous shower of organic detritus falling from upper layers of ocean.
4. **(a)** Contractile vacuole
   (b) **Any two from**: Water diffuses into cytoplasm of amoeba from surrounding medium; Water concentrated/pumped into contractile vacuole; Contractile vacuole empties into surrounding medium.
5. **Toxic chemicals** – PCB, DDT, other named pesticide or organochlorine **(1 mark). Plus any two from:** Chemical cannot be broken down in body of organism, stored in fatty deposits/organs; Small amounts in organisms lower in food chain do not cause harm; Concentration increases as reach higher trophic levels; Kills animals at top of food chain.

Pages 92–93

1. catalysts; chemical; conditions; denatured **(All correct for 2 marks)**
2. Protease – Protein; Lipase – Fat; Amylase – Carbohydrate
3. Enzymes within the washing powder **(1 mark)** digest stains **(1 mark)** Enzymes work best between 30–40°C so not all stains are removed at 20°C. **(1 mark)** Above 40°C enzymes are denatured/change shape so no stains removed. **(1 mark)**
4. 7 **should be ringed**
5. **(a)** Calcium chloride; Siphoned/drained
   (b) Continuous flow processing
   (c) Enzyme can be reclaimed/not wasted; Enzyme will not contaminate food product.
6. **(a)** Lactase
   (b) **Any two from**: Lactose enters large intestine undigested; Bacteria ferment the sugar; Diarrhoea and gas produced.
   (c) Glucose **and** galactose

Pages 94–95

1. Transgenic
2. **(a)** **Any two from**: Disease resistance; Pest resistance; Drought resistance; Herbicide resistance; Inclusion of additional vitamins.
   (b) **Any two from**: Organisms need to be cloned; Named method, e.g. adult cloning; Embryo transplantation; Cuttings; Tissue culture.

3. Enzymes 'cut' specific genes out of DNA/produce 'sticky ends'.
4. Marker gene inserted with desired gene into plasmid; Bacteria grown on agar plate containing antibiotic; Only transgenic bacteria survive and grow.
5. **(a)** The DNA at a crime scene can be compared with a suspect's DNA; A match can be found which is identical; The unique nature of DNA means that the system is almost foolproof as no one else in the world (apart from an identical twin) has that particular DNA fingerprint.
   (b) **Step 1**: Isolation – DNA extracted from person's tissue.
   Step 2: Fragmentation – DNA cut into fragments by restriction enzymes.
   Step 3: Separation – DNA segments separated by electrophoresis.
   Step 4: Comparison – DNA visualised and compared with DNA database using radioactive probes.
6. **Any two from**: Objections to access rights to the database – who is allowed to see it?; How long is the data held?; How secure is it?; Might samples be included when person has not committed a crime?; Invasion of privacy.

1. A meadow supports a wide variety of animals and plants. George is carrying out a survey of the meadow to assess the populations of organisms found there.

(a) State the term which describes the meadow as a place for organisms to live. [1]

....

(b) Which word describes the different populations in the meadow and their interaction with the physical factors found there? .... [1]

(c) George has laid pitfall traps in the meadow to capture and count soil invertebrates. He also notices that there are many flying insects which are too difficult to count and identify. Suggest an item of apparatus he could use to survey the flying insects. [1]

....

(d) George uses a 0.25 m^2 quadrat to survey the plant populations. He lays ten quadrats in one corner of the field and finds a mean count of 16 meadow buttercups. He estimates the area of the meadow to be 5000 m^2.

(i) Calculate the expected number of buttercups in the whole meadow. Show your working. [2]

....

....

(ii) Give **one** reason why George's estimate may be inaccurate. [1]

....

....

(e) George finds the two invertebrates shown below in his pitfall traps.

Beetle **Snail**

(i) The beetle feeds off other insects. Explain how the presence of a large number of beetles feeding off the same insects might affect the number of **beetles.** [2]

....

....

(ii) Thrushes eat snails and worms. Describe what would happen to the number of snails if large numbers of thrushes arrived in their habitat. [1]

....

[Total: .... / 9]

B4 Ecology in the Local Environment

Higher Tier

2. George wants to know more about the numbers of mammals in the meadow and lays some humane traps in the middle of the meadow to capture field voles. Eight hours later he checks the traps and finds 15 voles. He shaves a small section of fur off their backs and returns them to the meadow. He lays another set of traps. This time he catches 21 voles; four of these have shaved backs.

(a) Use this formula to calculate the number of field voles in the meadow.

$$\frac{\text{number in } 1^{st} \text{ sample} \times \text{number in } 2^{nd} \text{ sample}}{\text{number in } 2^{nd} \text{ sample previously marked}}$$

Show your working in the space below. [2]

....

....

(b) State **two** assumptions George might make when using this method. [2]

....

....

....

(c) George is not convinced that he has an accurate estimate of the number of field voles. Describe **two** ways he could improve the reliability of his estimate. [2]

....

....

....

[Total: .... / 6]

1. Glucose can be used by plants for energy or to build up bigger molecules. The diagram shows a starch molecule. The part labelled **A** is a glucose molecule.

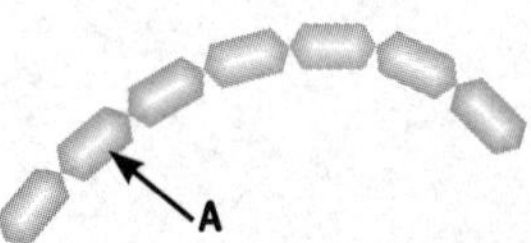

(a) In which organs of the plant would most of this starch be manufactured? [1]

....

(b) The plant can synthesise other molecules from the glucose it manufactures, such as cellulose and protein. State **one** use for each of these molecules. [2]

Cellulose ....

Protein ....

2. Write the **word** equation for photosynthesis. [2]

....

3. A market gardener puts a wood-burning stove in his greenhouse to increase the yield of his lettuces.

(a) Explain how this will increase the yield. [2]

....

....

(b) Suggest **one other** measure he could take to increase his yield. [1]

....

4. In the 17th century a Flemish scientist called Van Helmont carried out some experiments involving weighing the mass of a willow tree over five years. He found that the mass of the tree increased by over 30 times and yet the soil mass remained constant.

(a) If the tree had a starting mass of 120 g, calculate the finishing mass. Show your working. [2]

....

.... g

(b) Van Helmont concluded that the willow's mass was entirely due to water intake. Explain why Van Helmont was only partially correct. [1]

....

(c) What, apart from water, might the willow have absorbed from the soil? [1]

....

(d) Explain why this mass was hardly detectable. [1]

[Total: ...... / 13]

Higher Tier

5. A student decided that he would test a green plant to see how the rate of photosynthesis changed with temperature. The results he obtained are shown here.

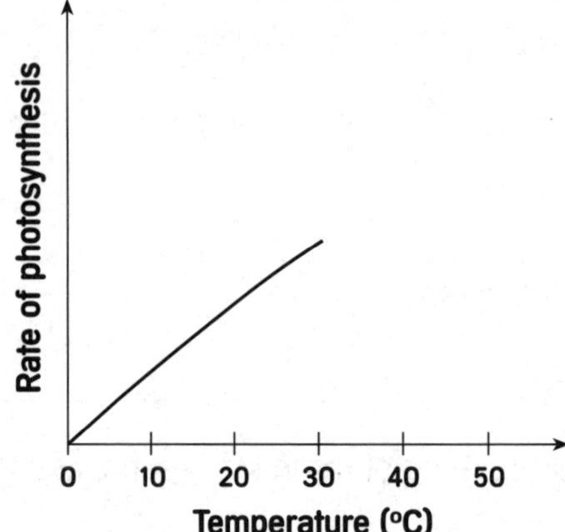

(a) He did not finish the experiment. Sketch on the graph the results you would expect him to have obtained. [1]

(b) Explain why photosynthesis varies with temperature over a range of 0°C to 50°C. [2]

6. The graph below shows how the rate of photosynthesis changed on two different days.

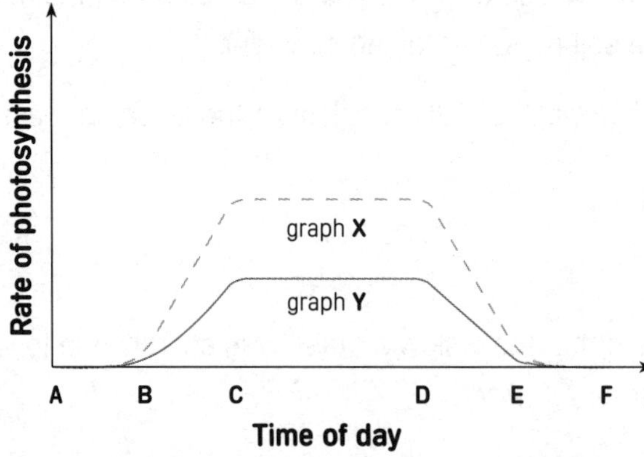

(a) Which graph, **X** or **Y**, represents a hot sunny day? ...... [1]

(b) Mark a **D** on the graph when dawn occurred, and an **N** to show when night occurred. [1]

[Total: ...... / 5]

1. This question is about leaves. Leaves are organs of photosynthesis. Below is a diagram showing a magnified view of the inside of a leaf. Three parts have been labelled. Label the remaining **three.** [3]

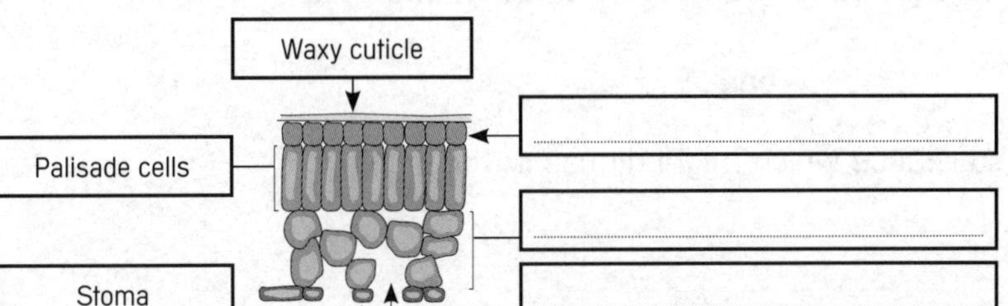

2. **(a)** Water is transported to the leaves from the roots. Give **two** reasons why water is needed in the leaves. [2]

....

....

(b) Describe the journey which excess water takes from a mesophyll cell to the outside atmosphere. In your answer, include ideas about **evaporation** and **diffusion**. [3]

....

....

....

[Total: .... /8]

Higher Tier

3. Leaves carry out photosynthesis very efficiently due to the many adaptations of the structures found within them. For each adaptation below explain the **advantage** this gives for efficient photosynthesis. [6]

Upper epidermis ....

....

Palisade cells ....

....

Spongy mesophyll ....

....

[Total: .... /6]

B4 Diffusion and Osmosis

1. Cells rely on diffusion as a means of transporting materials inwards and outwards.

   (a) Name **two** substances which move by diffusion **into** cells. [2]

   .... **and** ....

   (b) Name **one** substance which might diffuse **out** of a cell. [1]

   ....

2. Osmosis is a special case of diffusion involving water. Plants rely on osmosis for movement of materials around their various structures. Below is a diagram of three plant cells in the root of a plant. Cell **A** has a higher concentration of water than cell **C.**

   A B C

   Explain how water can move from cell **A** to cell **C.** [2]

   ....

   ....

3. Which of the following are examples of osmosis? Tick **(✓) three** correct options. [3]

   Water evaporating from leaves ☐

   Water moving from plant cell to plant cell ☐

   Mixing pure water and sugar solution ☐

   A pear losing water in a concentrated solution ☐

   Water moving from blood plasma to body cells ☐

   Sugar being absorbed from the intestine into the blood ☐

4. **(a)** Osmosis requires a partially permeable membrane to occur. Explain why sugar molecules cannot pass through a cell membrane but water molecules can. [1]

   ....

   (b) Blood cells also absorb and lose water by osmosis. Describe what the blood cells would look like in the following samples. You can use a labelled diagram to aid your description if you wish.

   (i) A normal blood sample where the red blood cells are bathed in plasma (which is the same concentration as their cytoplasm).

(ii) A blood sample from an athlete who has just run a marathon and is dehydrated.

(iii) A blood sample from a hospital patient who has accidentally been given a transfusion of pure water instead of saline. [3]

(i) **(ii)** **(iii)**

[Total: ______ / 12]

Higher Tier

5. Rabia is investigating how plant cells respond to being surrounded by different concentrations of solution. She places some rhubarb cells into pure water and then observes them under the microscope.

(a) Describe and explain the appearance of the rhubarb cells. [2]

(b) She then puts some rhubarb tissue into a strong salt solution. Describe how the cells would change in appearance if she observed them under the microscope again. [2]

(c) If a whole potted rhubarb plant was watered with a strong salt solution what would be the appearance of the plant after one hour? [1]

(d) Explain your answer to **(c)**. [2]

[Total: ______ / 7]

B4 Transport in Plants

1. This question is about transport in plants. Flowering plants have colonised all regions of the Earth and are very successful as organisms. They all share a basic structure consisting of four main organs.

   (a) For each organ, describe the function it performs in the plant. [4]

   Roots ....

   Stem ....

   Leaves ....

   Flowers ....

   (b) Label the different tube systems in the **root of a plant** in the diagram below. [2]

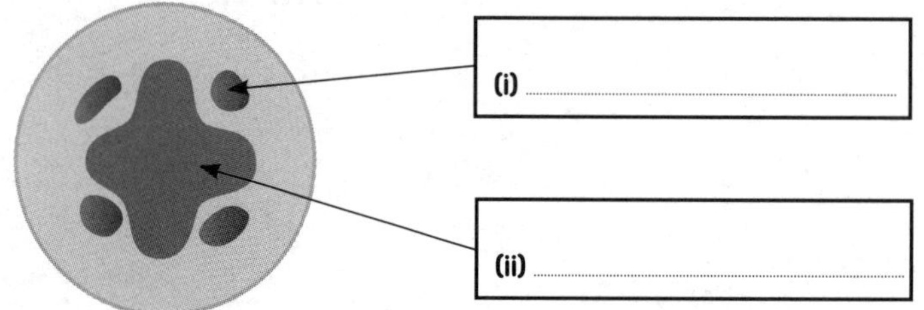

2. The diagram shows an experiment that can be carried out to investigate the water taken up by a plant. The results table is shown below.

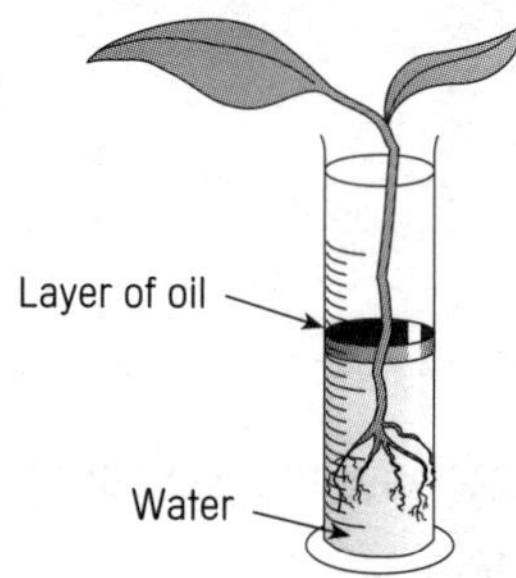

Time (in days)	**0**	**1**	**2**	**3**	**4**
Volume of water in cylinder (cm^3)	50	47	43	42	40

   (a) Explain why a layer of oil was poured on top of the water in the measuring cylinder. [1]

   ....

   (b) Calculate the average water loss per day. Show your working. [2]

   .... cm^3/day

   (c) Comment on the change in volume of water in the cylinder over the four days. [2]

   ....

   ....

(d) Suggest how the results would be different if: [3]

(i) the plant had been in a colder room. ....

(ii) the plant had been in a more humid atmosphere. ....

(iii) air had been blown over the leaves of the plant.

....

[Total: .... / 14]

Higher Tier

3. A celery stem contains vascular bundles. The vascular bundles contain xylem vessels which carry water and minerals. Describe **two** adaptations of xylem vessels which make them suited to the job they do. [2]

....

....

4. Guard cells respond to light intensity by regulating the rate at which water vapour is lost from the leaf by opening and closing. Explain how this occurs. In your answer, use ideas about osmosis and turgidity. [6]

✎ *The quality of your written communication will be assessed in this question.*

....

....

....

....

....

....

....

....

....

....

[Total: .... /8]

B4 Plants Need Minerals

1. A group of students investigated the effect that a mass of fertiliser would have on barley yield. They planted five fields of barley, adding differing amounts of fertiliser to each field. Five months later they measured the amount of barley produced in each field. The results are shown in the table below.

Mass of fertiliser used (kg)	0	50	100	150	200
Yield of barley (tonnes)	18	27	34	38	38

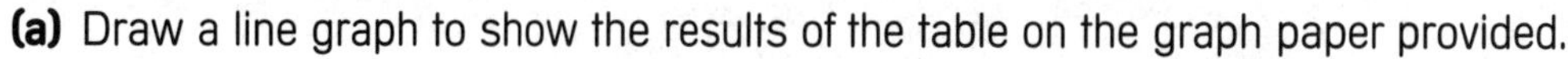

(a) Draw a line graph to show the results of the table on the graph paper provided. [3]

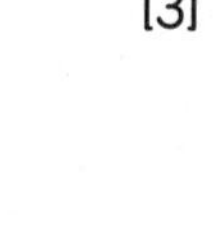

Yield (tonnes)

Mass of fertiliser (kg)

(b) State **two** variables the scientists needed to control to ensure that it was a fair test. [2]

....

....

(c) Which of the above fields was used as a 'control'? [1]

....

[Total: .... / 6]

Higher Tier

2. This question is about active transport. Minerals have to be absorbed by a plant against a concentration gradient from the soil.

(a) Name the specialised cells in the roots which are adapted for this function. [1]

....

(b) Explain how minerals are absorbed in these specialised cells. [2]

....

....

[Total: .... / 3]

1. The animal shown has recently died due to an infection. Already there are decomposers at work in its body. Name **two** factors that affect how quickly the animal will decompose. [2]

2. Decomposition can also affect the quality and safety of food. Below are listed four methods of food preservation. Describe how each one works to prevent the growth of decomposer microorganisms. [4]

Canning ....

Freezing ....

Pickling ....

Adding sugar ....

3. An experiment was set up to show how food decays. A nutrient solution was poured into two flasks. The necks were shaped and each flask was boiled. Flask **A** was then sealed and flask **B** was left open.

1 Pour a solution containing nutrients into flask **A**.

2 Melt and shape the neck of the flask.

3 Boil the nutrient solution to kill microorganisms and drive out air.

4 Seal the neck of the flask.

5 Pour more of the same nutrient solution into another flask (flask **B**). Repeat stages 2–3, but this time snap the neck of the flask off.

Flask **A**

Flask **A**

Flask **B**

(a) Which flask would show signs of decay first? .... [1]

(b) Explain your answer to **(a)**. [1]

(c) Explain why the flasks were boiled during the experiment. [1]

4. Detritivores make the decay process even faster.

(a) Name **two** examples of a detritivore. .... **and** .... [2]

(b) Explain how detritivores increase the rate of decay. [2]

5. Name **two** ways in which humans make use of decomposers. [2]

.... **and** ....

[Total: .... / 15]

Higher Tier

6. In an experiment, a known mass of toadstools were cultivated in compost with varying amounts of water. After five days, a sample of the toadstools from each were removed and the increase in dry mass was calculated. The results are shown below.

Water content of compost g/100 ml compost	5	10	15	20	25	30
Increase in dry mass of toadstools/%	0	7	9	15	21	22

(a) Toadstools are saprophytes. Explain what the term **saprophyte** means. [2]

(b) Describe the pattern of results obtained in the table. [2]

(c) Aisha concluded that 30 g of water per 100 ml compost was the optimum water content for growth of toadstools. Say whether you agree with her and give **one** reason. [2]

(d) Explain why the increase in **dry** mass was calculated and not the **wet** mass. [2]

[Total: .... / 8]

1. John is at the supermarket buying his weekly shop. He has recently made a decision to buy only organic products. At the fruit and vegetable section he chooses organic lettuce and broccoli because he does not approve of the use of inorganic chemicals such as pesticides in farming.

(a) State what a **pesticide** is. [1]

(b) State what a **herbicide** is. [1]

(c) Organic farmers do not use chemical pesticides or herbicides.

(i) Explain how they control weeds. [1]

(ii) Explain how they control insect pests. [1]

(d) Describe **two** methods organic farmers can employ to fertilise their crops as an alternative to inorganic fertilisers. [2]

2. A farmer breeds cows for beef. The animals are kept in enclosures inside a barn to regulate the temperature and to prevent the animals from moving around too much.

(a) In terms of food production, explain why the farmer would want to:

(i) regulate the temperature of the environment in which the cows are kept. [2]

(ii) restrict how much the cows move around. [1]

(b) Suggest **one other advantage** of keeping the cows inside a barn like this. [1]

(c) Suggest **one disadvantage** of raising cows in this way. [1]

(d) Some people object to livestock being raised in this way. Suggest **one** reason for this. [1]

3. Miriam grows tomatoes in huge greenhouses. She has a successful business as she can cut costs by using **hydroponics** to grow her plants.

(a) What is meant by the term **hydroponics**? [1]

(b) Explain why it is unlikely that John (**in Q1**) would approve of Miriam's methods. [1]

(c) The greenhouse environment enables Miriam to control the environmental conditions for fast, intensive growth. For each of the conditions below, explain how they might be controlled. [3]

Temperature

Light

Carbon dioxide

[Total: / 17]

Higher Tier

4. Describe **one further advantage,** and **one further disadvantage** of hydroponics as a system of growing plants. [2]

Advantage

Disadvantage

5. Pesticides can cause problems in food chains. Explain how these chemicals can accumulate in aquatic food chains. [3]

[Total: / 5]

1. The grasshopper is an insect and possesses an **exoskeleton**. It has to shed this as a 'skin' every time it is about to go through a growth phase. Humans have an endoskeleton. Describe **two other advantages** a human skeleton might have over an exoskeleton. [2]

....

....

2. Complete the following sentences. Choose words from the list below. [2]

external **chitin** **muscle** **cartilage** **earthworm** **wasp**

The simplest animals have no skeleton as such. For example, the .... has a fluid-filled cavity. More advanced invertebrates have an exoskeleton which is ....

This type of skeleton is made from .... and has to be shed as the animal grows.

Higher mammals have an endoskeleton which is made from bone and ....

3. David has had an accident while mountain biking. He is taken to hospital to have his arm X-rayed because his doctor believes he may have fractured it.

(a) Below is a diagram of a hollow bone from David's forearm. Write the names of the parts indicated on the diagram. [3]

(i) (ii) (iii)

(b) The X-ray is developed and shows that David has a **greenstick fracture**. Describe how the X-ray would be different if David had a **compound fracture**. [1]

....

(c) The **tendons in** David's arm have also been damaged. Explain why he may find it hard to move his fingers. [2]

....

....

4. Explain why bones are hollow. [2]

....

B5 Skeletons

5. These diagrams show two states which occur when bones move at the elbow joint.

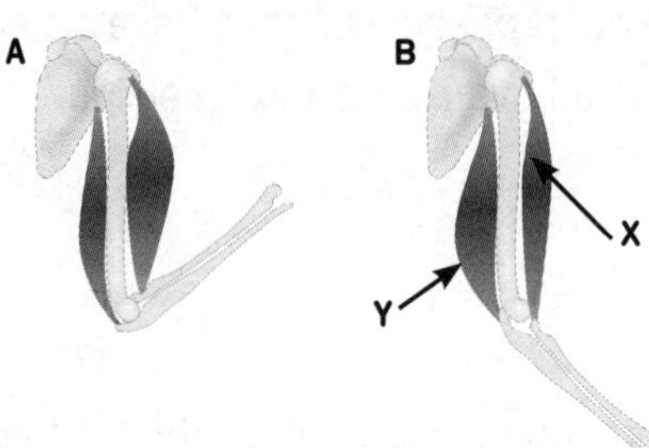

(a) What type of joint is the elbow joint? .... [1]

(b) Which diagram shows the joint extended – **A** or **B?** .... [1]

(c) Describe what has to happen to muscles **X** and **Y** for extension to happen. [2]

....

(d) What name is given to the process where muscles work against one another in this way? [1]

....

[Total: .... / 17]

Higher Tier

6. When the elbow joint moves it acts as a fulcrum. Explain how the idea of levers means that the attachment of muscles to bones gives an advantage. [2]

....

....

7. (a) Ann has a grandson who is only four weeks old. His skeleton, which has been largely cartilage, is growing fast. What name is given to the process where bone becomes harder? [1]

....

(b) Describe how this hardening process occurs. [2]

....

....

(c) The baby is taken to a clinic to check that he is healthy and growing. His height and weight are measured. How do scientists accurately measure the growth of an infant? [2]

....

....

[Total: .... / 7]

Circulatory Systems and the Cardiac Cycle B5

1. The pictures show a locust and a deer. Both have very different circulatory systems. Describe **two** features of each type of system.

(a) Locust – open circulatory system .... [2]

....

(b) Deer – closed circulatory system .... [2]

....

2. Saira is studying her heartbeat for a GCSE PE investigation. She measures her resting pulse rate.

(a) How will she do this? [2]

....

....

(b) She also takes her blood pressure.

(i) In which blood vessel will her pressure be greatest? .... [1]

(ii) What creates this high pressure? .... [1]

(c) (i) Saira has her heart monitored on an ECG machine. The trace appears normal. What exactly does an ECG measure? .... [1]

(ii) Name the machine which would detect sounds in Saira's heart. [1]

....

(d) Saira has her heart rate measured during a 200 m race. It doubles in rate. Explain why. [2]

....

....

B5 Circulatory Systems and the Cardiac Cycle

3. The heart is largely made of muscle, which is specialised to have an intrinsic rhythm. Intrinsic means that it can beat by itself without any input from the central nervous system. A group of cells called the **pacemaker** are located in the heart wall.

(a) Explain how these cells control the heartbeat. [1]

....

(b) If these cells stop working properly a surgical operation can be done to correct this. Describe what is done in this operation. [2]

....

....

[Total: .... / 15]

Higher Tier

4. The diagram shows a vertical section through the heart and illustrates how a wave of contraction results in a heartbeat. [2]

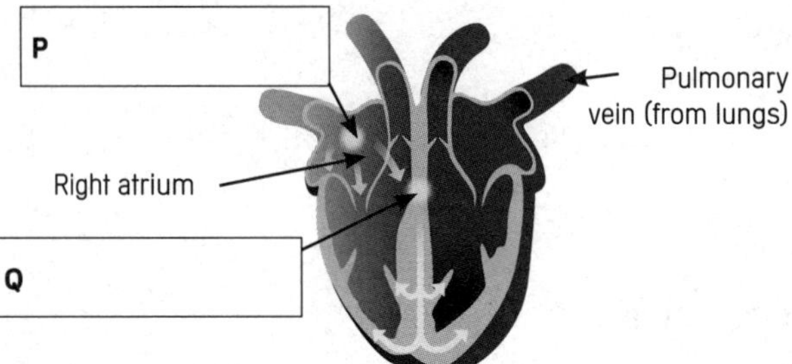

(a) Write down the names of **P** and **Q.**

(b) Describe the sequence of events which result in the heart pumping blood to the lungs and the rest of the body. Use the words below in your answer. [3]

arteries **veins** **ventricles** **valves** **atria**

....

....

....

5. Over thousands of years doctors and scientists have studied the circulatory system. Compare the views of the Ancient Greek doctor **Galen** with those of the 17th century doctor **Harvey**. [2]

....

....

[Total: .... / 7]

1. This question is about blood clotting. Shazni lives in a developing country and does not have access to a balanced diet. One result of this is that her blood does not clot properly.

(a) Explain why blood needs to clot. [1]

(b) To improve Shazni's poor clotting, which **two** nutrients might she need more of in her diet? [1]

(c) Unlike Shazni, Bradley lives in a developed country and has the opposite problem. His blood forms blood clots or **thromboses** too easily. He is prescribed an **anticoagulant**. Suggest what this anticoagulant might do. [1]

(d) Warfarin is a type of anticoagulant and in large doses can be fatal. This is why it is used in some rat poisons. The table shows some data from an experiment measuring the effect of different doses of warfarin in two samples of rat blood.

Warfarin dose/mg per kg body weight	Time for clot to form in sample 1	Time for clot to form in sample 2
0.2	52	61
0.4	101	99
0.6	193	197
0.8	300	311
1	978	984

(i) Calculate the average clotting time at 0.4 mg per kg of body weight. Show your working. [2]

(ii) Explain why the warfarin dose was measured in mg per kg of body weight. [1]

(iii) Describe the pattern of results shown in the data. [1]

(iv) Suggest **one** way in which this data could be unreliable. [1]

2. Benedict has decided to give blood. The assistant at the clinic reassures him that there is nothing to fear. He will give about 0.5 litres. He is found to be type AB negative.

(a) What might Benedict's blood be used for? .... [1]

(b) Before Benedict's blood is transfused, it is tested for problems. Suggest **one** problem it might be tested for. .... [1]

(c) Benedict's blood is carefully matched to the recipient before being transfused. What would happen to the donated blood if it was transfused into an incorrectly matched recipient? [1]

....

(d) Why might someone refuse to have a blood transfusion? [1]

....

[Total: .... / 12]

Higher Tier

3. A patient in hospital requires a blood transfusion. She is blood group O.

(a) Which blood group-related antibodies will be circulating in her blood? [1]

....

(b) Which is the only blood group she can receive blood from? .... [1]

(c) The patient had been involved in a car accident where she sustained some severe lacerations (cuts). Describe the process and biological molecules which would act in her blood to ensure clotting. [2]

....

....

4. All human foetuses are born with a hole in the heart, which means that the lungs are almost completely bypassed.

(a) Where does the foetus obtain its oxygen from? .... [1]

(b) If this hole does not close properly at birth then the individual may have symptoms of breathlessness. Explain what causes this. [1]

....

(c) What is done to remedy this problem? [1]

....

[Total: .... / 7]

1. Scientists are studying the performance of pearl divers living on a Japanese island. They have taken measurements of the lungs of five 20–30 year-olds and timed how long they can stay underwater. The scientists also measured recovery time for the divers' breathing rates after a dive. The data is shown in the table below.

Vital capacity/litres	Max. time under water/mins	Time for breathing rate recovery/mins
3.5	2.5	3.2
4.0	2.7	2.9
4.3	2.8	3.5
4.5	2.9	2.8
4.6	3.0	2.5

(a) What is meant by the term **vital capacity**? [1]

....

(b) One of the team of scientists suggests that having a larger vital capacity allows a diver to stay underwater for longer. Do you agree with her? Give a reason for your answer. [2]

Agree/disagree ....

Reason ....

....

(c) Another member of the team says that they ought to have investigated the divers' respiration rates also. What is the difference between **breathing** and **respiration**? [1]

....

(d) The scientists think that the data about breathing recovery rate is inconclusive. Suggest how more valid data could be obtained. [2]

....

....

(e) An MRI scan is taken of a diver's chest cavity. The image produced is enhanced and shown below.

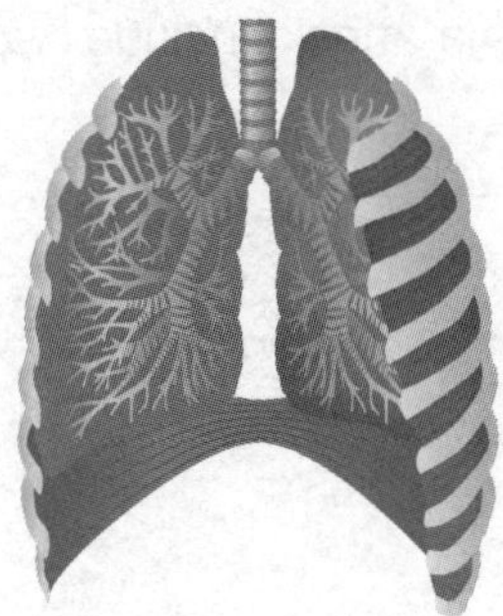

(i) Label the **diaphragm** with an **X**. [1]

(ii) Describe and explain how the diaphragm works to cause **inspiration** in the diver. [2]

....

....

(f) A spirometer trace is taken of the divers. The resulting trace of one diver is shown below. Using the graph, work out the tidal volume. [1]

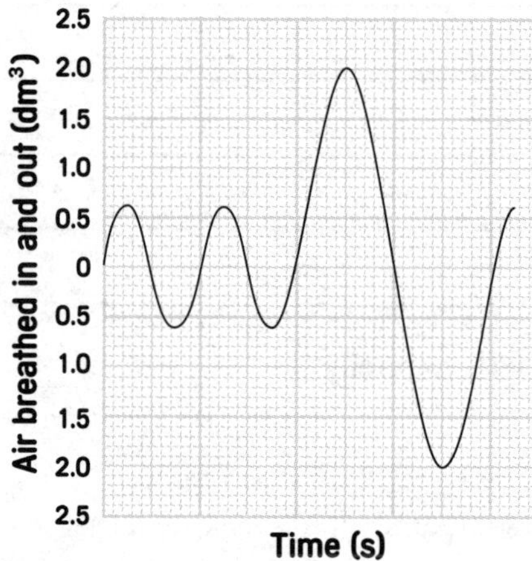

....

2. The diagram shows a layer of cells from the trachea.

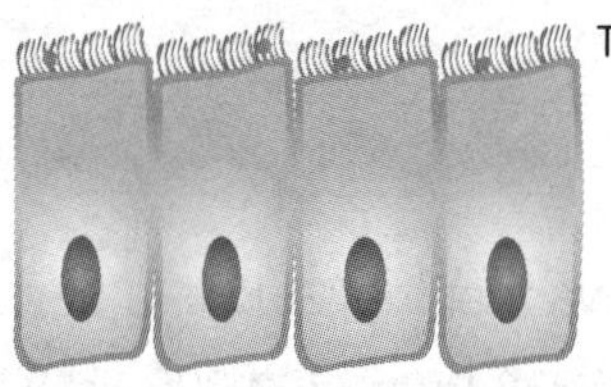

Explain how the cells are adapted for preventing entry of foreign particles into the soft tissue of the lungs. [2]

....

....

[Total: .... / 12]

Higher Tier

3. Describe what happens in an asthma attack. Include **two** symptoms in your answer. [3]

....

....

....

[Total: .... / 3]

1. Crohn's disease is a disease of the intestines that causes them to become inflamed. There are many symptoms including abdominal pain, diarrhoea, vomiting and weight loss. A sufferer is having a hospital procedure called a barium meal, which allows doctors to view the intestines as the barium shows up very clearly on a radiograph.

(a) Locate the large intestine on the diagram and label it with an **X**. [1]

(b) Label the stomach with a **Y**. [1]

(c) An inflamed large intestine does not absorb water very well. State which symptom of Crohn's disease may result from this. Give a reason for your answer. [2]

Symptom ....

Reason ....

[Total: ...... / 4]

Higher Tier

2. The small intestine is adapted for the efficient absorption of food. Explain how the small intestine achieves this.

✎ *The quality of your written communication will be assessed in this question.* [6]

....

....

....

....

....

....

....

....

....

....

[Total: ...... / 6]

B5 Waste Disposal

1. Tan-mu is exercising. Many changes are happening in her body. Sweat glands help to control her body temperature.

(a) Write about how the sweat glands help to control the temperature of her body. [2]

....

....

(b) As Tan-mu exercises she produces carbon dioxide in her cells. What name is given to the process which converts substances into waste products? [1]

....

(c) Tan-mu's liver produces urea. Which substances are changed to form the urea? [1]

....

(d) Tan-mu's kidneys process the urea. The route the urea follows is shown in the sequence below. Fill in the **two** boxes with the missing stages. [2]

[Total: .... / 6]

Higher Tier

(e) The diagram shows one of Tan-mu's kidney tubules.

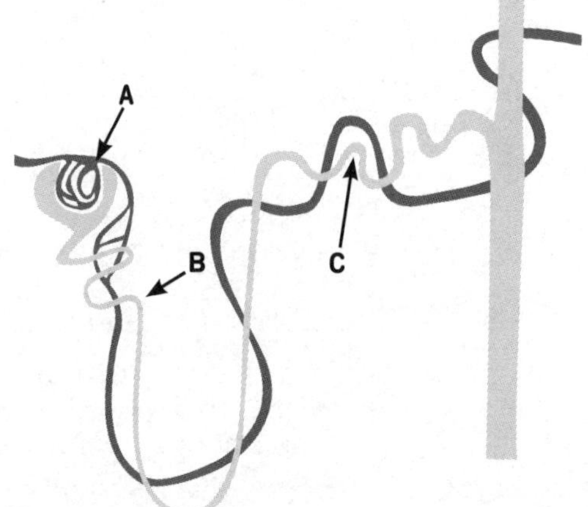

(i) In which region does **ultrafiltration** occur (**A**, **B** or **C**)? .... [1]

(ii) Where does **selective reabsorption** occur (**A**, **B** or **C**)? .... [1]

(iii) Where does salt regulation occur (**A**, **B** or **C**)? .... [1]

(iv) Explain how the brain and kidneys work together to restore water levels in the blood when the body is dehydrated. [3]

....

....

....

2. Dialysis machines are used when people suffer kidney failure and need urea removed from their blood artificially.

(a) Name another substance which the dialysis machine will regulate. [1]

....

(b) Explain how the dialysis machine extracts urea but does not allow useful substances to be lost from the patient's blood. [3]

....

....

....

[Total: .... / 10]

B5 Life Goes On

1. Give **two** reasons why a couple may not be able to conceive. [2]

2. The graph below shows the thickness of the uterus during the course of the menstrual cycle. Use the graph to explain what happens between days 5 and 28. [3]

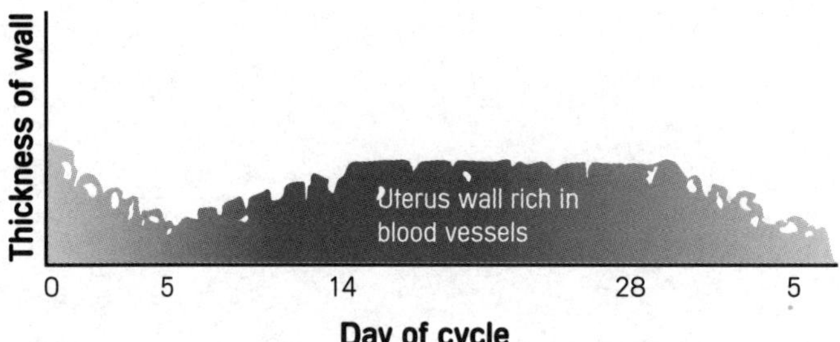

3. Fertilisation and pregnancy are not guaranteed for every couple who want to have a baby. One possible treatment for infertility is IVF.

(a) Describe how IVF is different to normal fertilisation. [1]

(b) The prospective mother is often given a fertility drug prior to IVF.

(i) What is likely to be contained in this drug? [1]

(ii) The resulting embryos are implanted into the mother's uterus. Give **one** drawback of this technique. [1]

(c) There are alternatives available to couples who have difficulty conceiving. For each of the methods below, describe what is involved. [3]

Artificial insemination

Egg donation

Surrogacy ....

....

4. Foetal screening allows the progress of a pregnancy to be monitored. In addition, if the mother is 40 years of age or older, she can choose to have an **amniocentesis**.

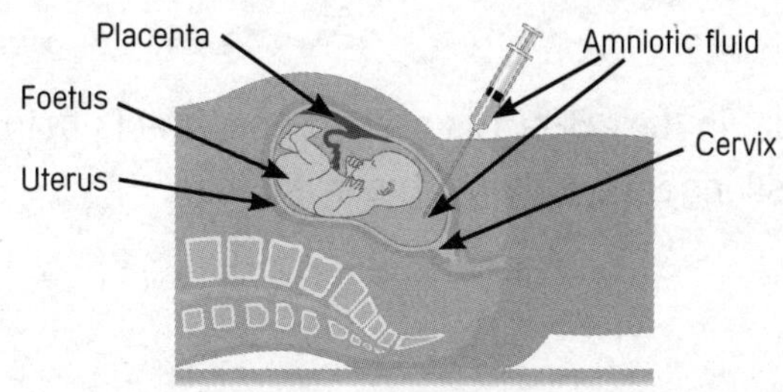

(a) Use the diagram to describe what is involved in an amniocentesis. [2]

....

....

(b) If amniocentesis is positive for an abnormality then the couple is faced with difficult decisions.

(i) Discuss the options open to the couple under these circumstances. [2]

....

....

(ii) Why might some people choose not to have an amniocentesis? [1]

....

[Total: .... / 16]

Higher Tier

5. Explain how fertility can be reduced by use of the contraceptive pill. In your answer, name any hormones involved. [2]

....

....

....

[Total: .... / 2]

B5 Growth and Repair

1. Jordan is a rapidly growing teenager. His father and mother are both very tall and Jordan believes that with this parentage he will be tall enough to make the local basketball team.

(a) Write down **two other** factors, apart from his parents' genes, which can affect Jordan's height and weight. [1]

(b) Jordan's grandparents are in their 80s. His great grandparents both died in their 70s. Explain why human life expectancy is longer now than it has ever been. [2]

2. This question is about organ donation. Alfred is 43 years old and has been on dialysis for two years. He has recently been offered a kidney transplant.

(a) Suggest why Alfred has had to wait a long time for a kidney to become available. [1]

(b) Alfred could not have a mechanical replacement for his damaged kidneys. Explain why not. [1]

(c) The kidney Alfred receives was donated by the victim of a road traffic accident. The victim carried a donor card. What additional consent is needed before the organ can be donated? [1]

[Total: .... / 6]

Higher Tier

3. **(a)** Why must organ recipients take immuno-supressive drugs for the rest of their lives? [1]

(b) Explain the problems connected with taking these drugs. [1]

4. **(a)** There are two approaches to creating an organ donor register: an 'opt-in' system in which people volunteer to be on the register, or an 'opt-out' system where people have to say if they don't want to be donors. Give a **disadvantage** of the opt-in system. [1]

(b) Suggest a reason why relatives of a person on the National Register of Donors might not agree to let the donation go ahead. [1]

5. The table below contains a record of a girl's height from birth to age 22.

Age (years)	0	2	4	6	8	10	12	14	16	18	20	22
Height (cm)	55	90	107	122	134	147	159	168	170	170	170	170

(a) Use the figures from the table to draw a graph of the girl's height from birth to age 22. [3]

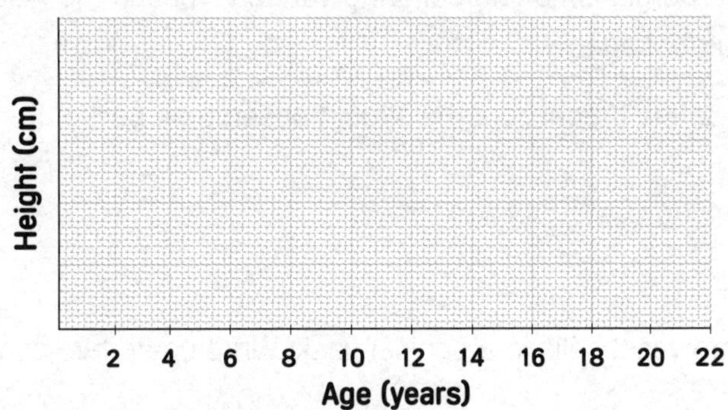

(b) Between which ages did she grow fastest? [1]

(c) By what age had she stopped growing completely? [1]

6. **(a)** Give an example of a problem that occurs as a result of longer life expectancy. [1]

(b) Explain how your answer to **(a)** can impact on society. [2]

[Total: / 12]

B6 Understanding Microbes

1. The diagram shows the structure of a typical bacterium. Two parts have been labelled.

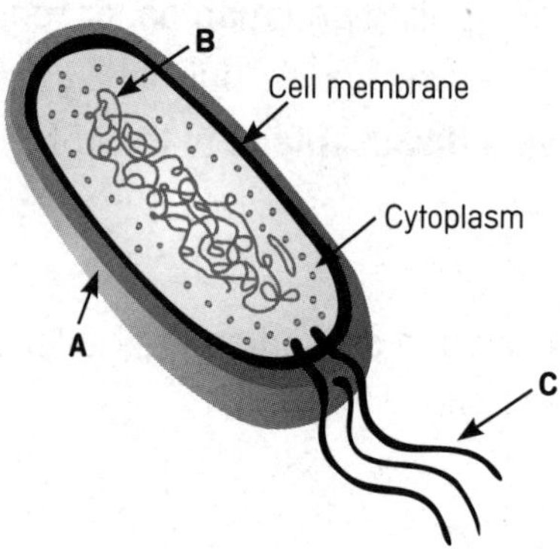

(a) Name parts **A**, **B** and **C**. [3]

A .... **B** .... **C** ....

(b) Describe the function of part **C**. [1]

....

2. Majid is studying microorganisms and culturing various types in the laboratory. He decides to grow some bacteria on nutrient agar.

(a) Write down **two** safety precautions he should observe as part of his aseptic technique. [2]

....

....

(b) Majid grows some yeast cells in a conical flask. Write down **two** conditions that will help the yeast grow rapidly. [2]

....

....

(c) Majid removes a drop of the yeast culture and views the cells under a microscope. He notices that some cells are reproducing.

(i) Sketch the appearance of a yeast cell reproducing. [2]

(ii) On your diagram, label the structure which will carry the genetic information for the new cell. Mark this with an **X**. [1]

(d) Explain why Majid will not be able to culture viruses using the above two techniques. [1]

....

[Total: .... / 12]

Higher Tier

3. Describe **two** ways in which bacteria can obtain food. [2]

4. The graph below shows the progress of yeast growth at **35°C** and **25°C**.

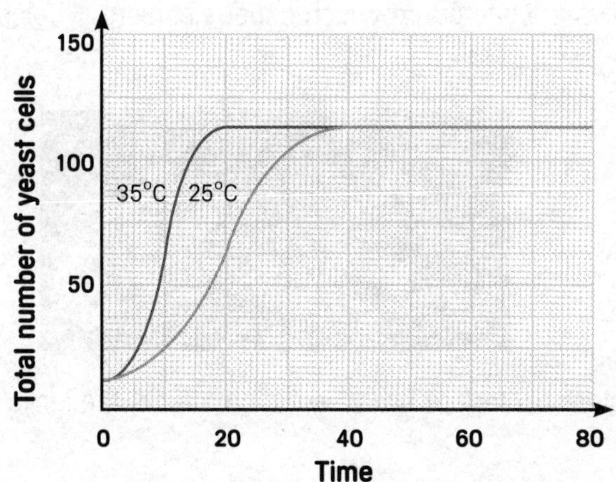

(a) Sketch a further curve on the graph to show how the growth would differ at 15°C. [2]

(b) Explain why growth would slow down above 40°C. [1]

(c) Use the graph to predict how many yeast cells there would be in the culture if it was left at 35°C for 20 days. [1]

(d) These growth curves follow a typical 'S' shape. Explain the shape of the curves in terms of what is happening to the yeast cells. [3]

[Total: ____ / 9]

B6 Harmful Microorganisms

1. Microorganisms consist of bacteria, viruses, fungi and protozoa. Many cause harm to the human body.

   (a) Write down the term that describes such organisms. [1]

   ....

   (b) Microbes can enter the body through various routes. Describe **two** of these routes. [2]

   ....

   ....

2. The picture below shows the bacterium which causes cholera. Cholera is widespread in areas where natural disasters occur.

   (a) What does the cholera bacterium produce which affects the large intestine? [1]

   ....

   (b) Explain, giving **two** reasons, why cholera spreads rapidly in natural disaster zones. [2]

   ....

   ....

   (c) Severe cases of cholera can be treated with **antibiotics**. Explain why an **antiseptic** would not be effective. [1]

   ....

3. During human history there have been times when the fight against disease has made significant steps forward. For each scientist, name the breakthrough which they were responsible for and how it was used. [6]

   Fleming ....

   ....

   Lister ....

   ....

   Pasteur ....

   ....

[Total: .... / 13]

Higher Tier

4. The graph shows data from hospitals in Australia during 2007 and 2008.

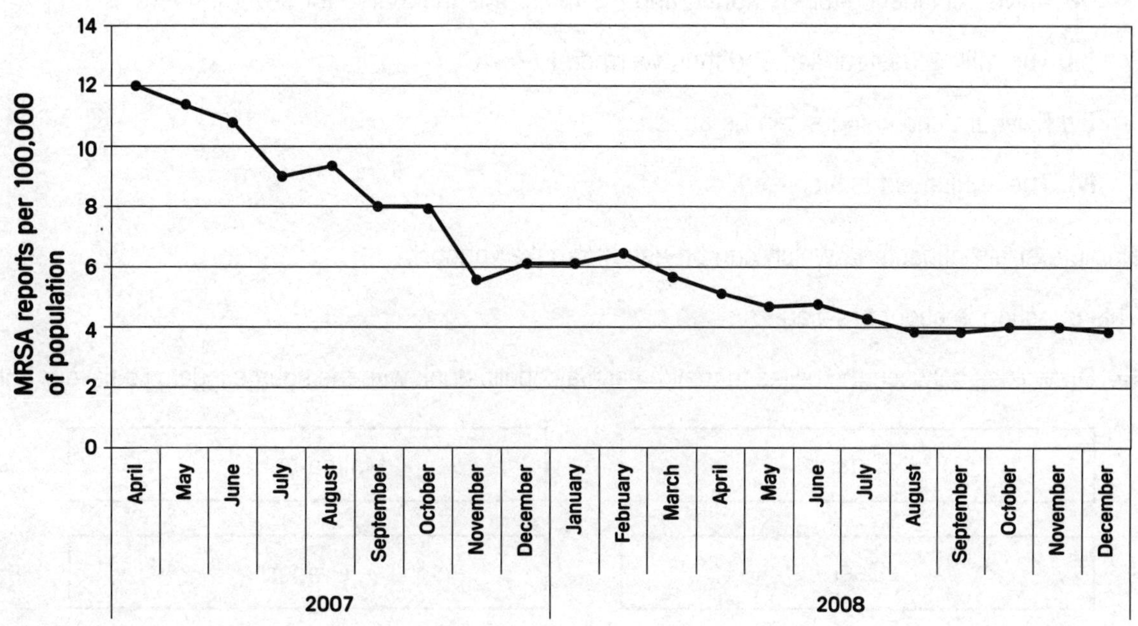

(a) Describe the trend shown in the graph. [2]

....

....

(b) Give **one** reason why so called 'superbugs' have become more of a problem in recent years. [1]

....

(c) Suggest a reason for the overall trend shown. [1]

....

[Total: .... / 4]

B6 Useful Microorganisms

1. **(a)** The stages of making yoghurt are given below, but they are not in the right order. Number the boxes to put them in the correct order. [5]

   (i) The bacteria reproduce and feed on the lactose sugar in the milk, turning it into lactic acid. ☐

   (ii) A live bacterial culture is added and the mixture is incubated for several hours. ☐

   (iii) The milk is pasteurised and then warmed to 40°C. ☐

   (iv) Flavours and colours can be added. ☐

   (v) The equipment is sterilised. ☐

(b) Name a strain of bacteria which can be used to make yoghurt. .... [1]

2. This question is about brewing.

   (a) Draw lines between the boxes to match each alcoholic drink with the source it gets its flavour from. [1]

Cider	Malted barley
Beer	Grapes
Wine	Apples

   (b) Write down the **word** equation for fermentation. [1]

   ....

   (c) This picture shows copper fermentation vats in a brewery.

   (i) Explain why these vats are sealed. [1]

   ....

   (ii) A chemical is added straight after the fermentation stage. Explain the purpose of this chemical. [1]

   ....

   (iii) Two stages remain in this process. Describe what happens in these **two** stages. [1]

   ....

   ....

3. Explain why spirit drinks are distilled. [1]

   ....

4. Yeast is able to use sugar as a basis for respiration. Explain how this property can be made use of in food-processing factories. [1]

5. Some beers are manufactured to be less 'fizzy' so that they complement meals such as curries. Explain how the brewing vessels would have to be altered to allow this to occur. [2]

[Total: ...... / 15]

Higher Tier

6. **(a)** Write down the balanced **symbol** equation for fermentation. [2]

(b) Explain what would be formed if yeast were allowed to respire **with** oxygen present. [1]

(c) This graph shows how the amount of carbon dioxide produced by respiring yeast (in five minutes) is affected by temperature.

(i) Use the graph to find the volume of carbon dioxide produced at 35°C. [1]

(ii) Use the graph to find the optimum temperature for yeast activity. [1]

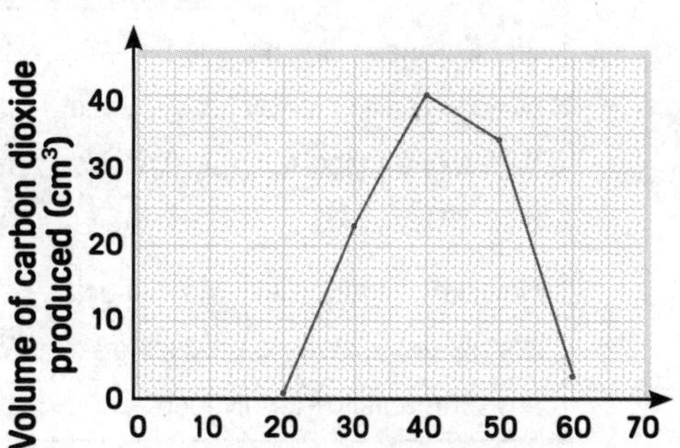

(d) Explain what is involved in the pasteurisation of beer. [2]

(e) Why might a brewer want to use yeast cultures which have a greater tolerance to alcohol? [1]

[Total: ...... / 8]

B6 Biofuels

1. The diagram on the right shows a digester which can make use of human sewage. The gas produced from this vessel contains a mixture of 60% methane and 40% carbon dioxide.

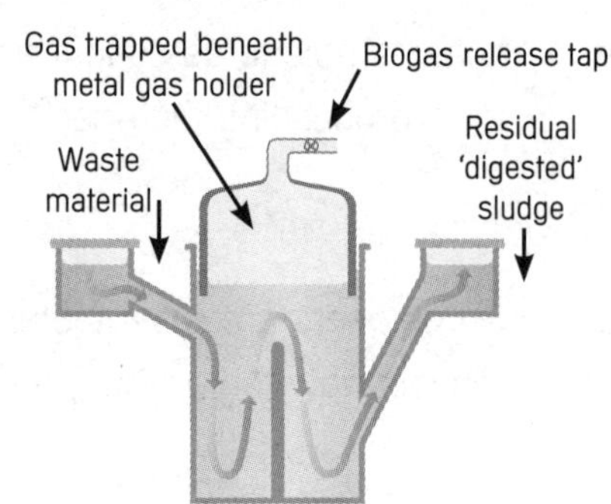

(a) Give the name of this type of biofuel. [1]

....

(b) This type of digester is described as a **continuous flow** digester. Explain what this means. [2]

....

....

(c) Give **two** uses of this biofuel. .... [2]

....

(d) Explain why these types of digesters are useful in remote parts of the world. [1]

....

2. Here is an extract about 'gasohol' from a newspaper.

Biofuels are 'deforestation diesel'

The European Union issued a directive calling for biofuels to meet 5.75% of transportation fuel needs by 2010.

However, some believe that biofuels are not the answer to producing environmentally friendly fuel.

The grain needed to fill the petrol tank of an SUV with ethanol could feed one person for a year. Assuming the petrol tank is refilled every two weeks, the amount of grain needed would feed a hungry Ethiopian village for a year.

Much of the fuel that Europeans use will be imported from Brazil, where the Amazon is being burned to plant more sugar and soya beans. This is destroying the rainforest habitat of orang-utans and many other species. Species are dying for our driving.

(a) What is ethanol mixed with to produce 'gasohol'? .... [1]

(b) One of the advantages of growing plants for biofuel is that the process is **carbon-neutral**. Explain what this means. [2]

....

....

(c) Describe **one other** advantage of biofuels. [1]

....

[Total: .... / 10]

Higher Tier

3. **(a)** Biogas has to contain more than 50% methane to burn easily. What happens if the content falls below 10% methane? [1]

....

(b) Specialised bacteria are needed to break down the fats and proteins in the digester.

Name **two** products which would result from this breakdown. [2]

.... **and** ....

(c) Explain why the temperature of the digester needs to be kept optimal. [2]

....

....

4. A Swiss biotech firm is developing genetically engineered maize that can help convert itself into ethanol by growing a particular enzyme. This means that the maize does not need to be processed industrially to the same extent. Use your knowledge of genetic modification and the greenhouse effect to compare the **advantages** and **disadvantages** of this development.

✎ *The quality of your written communication will be assessed in this question.* [6]

....

....

....

....

....

....

....

....

....

....

[Total: .... / 11]

B6 Life in Soil

1. (a) Which word best describes an earthworm's mode of nutrition? Place a (ring) round the correct answer. [1]

   saprophyte **decomposer** **detritivore** **producer** **consumer**

   (b) Explain how earthworms increase the fertility, structure and drainage of the soil. [3]

2. Match the soils below with their characteristics. Join the boxes with lines. [1]

Clay	Large mineral particles
Sandy	Small mineral particles
Loam	Mixture of clay and sand

3. Jack was carrying out an experiment on his garden soil. He wanted to know the water content, so he carried out the following steps:

   1. Weigh and record soil sample → **2.** Heat sample in oven to evaporate water → **3.** Re-weigh sample

   Jack obtained the following results:

   Mass of soil before heating: 52.3 g **Mass of soil after heating:** 42.4 g

   (a) Calculate the percentage water content of the soil sample. Show your working. [2]

   (b) Jack's friend, Mikael, said that Jack's result was incorrect. Suggest a further step Jack could take to ensure the accuracy of his result. [2]

   (c) Jack also wanted to find the **humus** content of his sample. What is humus? [1]

(d) Describe a method Jack could follow to find the humus content of the sample. [2]

[Total: ______ / 12]

Higher Tier

4. Explain why sandy soil is very porous. [2]

5. Here is a soil food chain.

plant roots ⟶ **wire worms** ⟶ **?** ⟶ **moles**

(a) Suggest an organism which could occupy the missing space (**?**) in the food chain. [1]

(b) In terms of feeding, what type of organism is a wire worm? [1]

(c) Explain why there are always more herbivores than carnivores in a food chain. [3]

6. **(a)** Describe **one** consequence for plants which are planted in acid soil. [1]

(b) Write down **one** method which farmers can use to adjust the pH of acid soil. [1]

[Total: ______ / 9]

B6 Microscopic Life in Water

1. Lakeside is a nature reserve consisting of a freshwater lake and surrounding deciduous woodland. The lake contains a rich diversity of plant and animal life. The surrounding water prevents the bodies of organisms from dehydrating.

(a) Write down **one other advantage** of living in an aquatic habitat. [1]

....

(b) Grass snakes can swim in water but also crawl on the land. They are adapted for air breathing. Describe **one advantage** of breathing air over having to breathe water as a fish does. [2]

....

....

(c) Phytoplankton are microscopic plants that live in water. Write down the name of the microscopic animals that feed off them. [1]

....

(d) The reserve staff are in the process of advising a nearby farmer about fertiliser run-off from his fields.

(i) Explain how this run-off will affect the plant life in the lake. [4]

....

....

....

....

(ii) Write down **one other** factor that will affect the plant life. [1]

....

(e) Detergents polluting the lake have also been detected. Suggest a source for this pollutant. [1]

....

(f) To detect water quality in the lake, the reserve staff made use of **biological indicators**. Describe how these indicators can be used. In your answer you should: [3]

- Give **two** examples of organisms used.
- Name **one other** pollutant other than detergent or fertilisers that could affect the water quality.
- Describe how the biodiversity of the organisms is affected by pollution.

....

....

....

2. Here is a marine food chain.

plankton ⟶ **krill** ⟶ **penguin** ⟶ **seal** ⟶ **killer whale**

(a) Name an organism in this food chain which is a carnivore. .... [1]

(b) In your answer to **Q1.(c)** there were two types of plankton identified. In the space below, sketch a **pyramid of biomass** which shows the feeding relationship between these two types of plankton in **winter**. [2]

[Total: .... / 16]

Higher Tier

3. Describe what is meant by the term **marine snow**. [1]

....

4. The amoeba has to carry out all of its processes of life within the space of one cell. One of these functions is **osmoregulation**.

(a) Name the structure within the amoeba which carries out osmoregulation. [1]

....

(b) Explain how this structure helps the amoeba cope with living in a freshwater environment. [2]

....

....

5. Pollutants can build up in the bodies of aquatic organisms through a process called **biomagnification**. Explain how this occurs. In your answer you should:

- name a toxic chemical which can accumulate in this way.
- explain why the chemical accumulates. [3]

....

....

....

....

[Total: .... / 7]

B6 Enzymes in Action

1. Complete the following sentences about enzymes. Use the correct words from the list below. [2]

killed **catalysts** **digested** **carbohydrates** **physical**
chemical **conditions** **ranges** **denatured**

Enzymes are biological .... which control .... reactions in living systems. They have many applications in industry but require the correct .... to work in. For example, if the temperature is too high they become .... and functionless.

2. Draw lines between the boxes to match each enzyme to the stain it breaks down. [1]

Protease	Fat
Lipase	Carbohydrate
Amylase	Protein

3. Selena carries out an experiment with a biological washing powder. She produces some pieces of cotton cloth with a number of stains dried on them. Each piece of cloth is put in a beaker with 250 ml of water of different temperatures for 30 minutes. The results after 30 minutes are shown below.

Water at 20°C **Water at 37 °C** **Water at 70°C**

Explain these results. [4]

....

....

....

4. Ring the pH which most enzymes work best at. [1]

1 **4** **7** **8** **12**

5. This question is about immobilised enzymes. The process below shows how an enzyme can be immobilised and used.

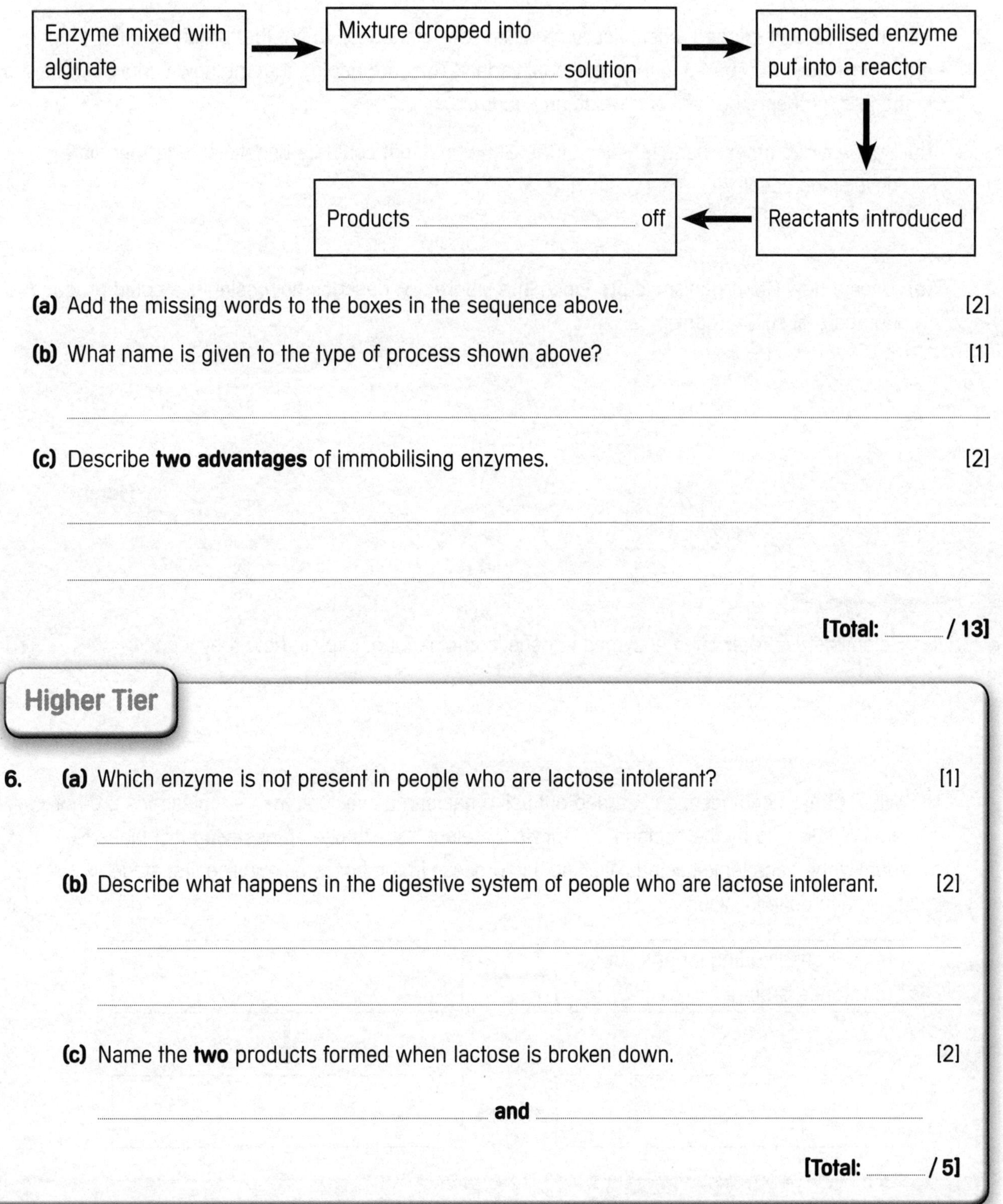

(a) Add the missing words to the boxes in the sequence above. [2]

(b) What name is given to the type of process shown above? [1]

______

(c) Describe **two advantages** of immobilising enzymes. [2]

______

______

[Total: ____ / 13]

Higher Tier

6. **(a)** Which enzyme is not present in people who are lactose intolerant? [1]

______

(b) Describe what happens in the digestive system of people who are lactose intolerant. [2]

______

______

(c) Name the **two** products formed when lactose is broken down. [2]

______ **and** ______

[Total: ____ / 5]

B6 Gene Technology

1. Write down the name given to an organism which receives a gene from another species. [1]

....

2. Scientists have developed a genetically modified (GM) variety of wheat that produces 50% bigger grains in a head compared to the traditional variety. They are hoping that the new variety can be grown in the arid, nutrient-poor soil of developing countries.

   (a) Suggest **two other** characteristics of the GM wheat that could be beneficial to farmers in a developing country. [1]

   .... **and** ....

   (b) Once a new GM organism is produced in a laboratory, describe how scientists could produce large numbers of such organisms. [2]

   ....

   ....

[Total: .... / 4]

Higher Tier

3. Scientists use **restriction** enzymes in genetic engineering. Explain how they work. [1]

....

....

4. When genetic engineering is carried out using bacteria as vectors, the new plasmids are not always taken up by the bacteria. Scientists therefore have to use an **assaying** technique to identify the transgenic bacteria. Outline this process in the boxes below. The first stage has been done for you. [3]

Marker gene coding for antibiotic resistance is obtained	→	
		↓
	←	

5. This question is about DNA fingerprinting. The diagram shows a banding system of genes produced from the DNA fingerprinting process.

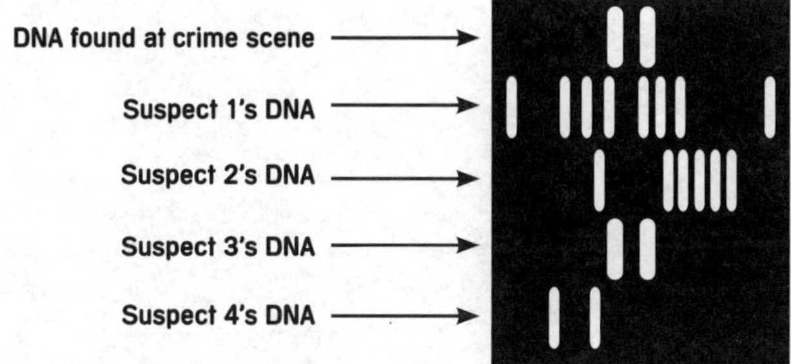

(a) Explain how forensic scientists can use this to identify a suspect. In your answer, state why this type of evidence is almost 'foolproof'. [3]

....

....

....

(b) Outline the steps taken to obtain a DNA fingerprint. [4]

Step 1 ....

....

Step 2 ....

....

Step 3 ....

....

Step 4 ....

....

6. Discuss why some people object to DNA fingerprints being held on a national database. [2]

....

....

[Total: .... / 13]

Notes

Notes

Notes

